GETTING IT

**Seven Rules and Other Useful Tidbits
For Life and Business**

GETTING IT

**Seven Rules and Other Useful Tidbits
For Life and Business**

**Written by
Pat O'Connor**

Phase Publishing, LLC
Seattle

If you purchased this book without a cover, you should be aware that this book is stolen property. It was reported as "unsold and destroyed" to the publisher, and neither the author nor the publisher has received any payment for this "stripped" book.

Text copyright © 2024 by Pat O'Connor
Cover art copyright © 2024 by POC Media, Inc.

All rights reserved. Published by Phase Publishing, LLC in collaboration with POC Media, Inc. No part of this book may be reproduced or transmitted in any form, or by any means, electronic or mechanical, including photocopying or recording or by any information storage and retrieval system, without written permission from the publisher.

Phase Publishing, LLC first paperback edition
October 2024

ISBN 978-1-952103-71-1
Library of Congress Control Number 2024945017
Cataloging-in-Publication Data on file.

Name: Patrick L. O'Connor

Title: Getting It

Wayne, PA: POC Media, Inc.

Identifiers:

Subjects: Life | Business | Philosophy | Spirituality | Self-Help

Forward

by Dr. Robert Melillo
Clinician, Brain Researcher, Professor
8x best-selling author of *Disconnected Kids*
Co-Founder of Brain Balance Achievement Centers

In this era of Instagram, Facebook, Tik Tok, and various flavors of social media, there is no shortage of individuals who claim to know the "secret to success," of course, for a price. There is a plethora of life coaches, and no shortage of books or podcasts about personal and professional development.

Many people ask for my advice, and I tell them that the single most important thing that one can do as one begins a journey of personal development is to be careful who one takes advice from. I am a researcher. When I am writing a research paper and searching for scientific references, the quality of the references and the quality of the journal where it was published matters. A paper being published in a peer-reviewed journal is no guarantee of accuracy or validity. One must always check references. When one is about to invest time and money into following recommendations, one must ask:

- Who is this author or advisor?
- What have they accomplished in their life?
- Have they been successful in the field for which they are advising?
- Do they practice what they preach?

There are countless people who write books and sell courses without experiencing any real-world success. I know people who have become "life coaches," whose own personal lives are a mess. They may take a course and be certified, but they have never achieved any measure of success and are poorly equipped to teach others.

It's also vital to be able to accurately define "success." Most coaches are focused on financial success or acquiring followers. True success is measured based on the person one becomes, the value one adds to the world, and the example we set for those around us.

In a Harvard study that lasted seventy-five years, the college followed their graduates as well as young men that grew up in the less affluent neighborhoods of Boston. After decades of empirical results, the most important factor in health and happiness was interpersonal relationships. The quality of relationships, especially with one's significant other and children, is the truest measure of happiness and success.

The manner of one's success matters. Some of the wealthiest and most financially successful people in the world have horrible relationships and have lost the love and respect of their own children.

Before reading a book or taking a course, I first consider the quality of the person writing the book, both inside and outside of business. Has the author earned the respect of those around him or her? Have they ever lost out on financial gain to keep their word; have they ever sacrificed their own time and wealth for the benefit of others; have they made a difference in the world beyond their own bank account?

From a spiritual perspective, does the author have a connection to a higher power; does he or she believe that there is a reason for things beyond what they can see. Do they tap into the creative force of the universe, in whatever form they choose to believe such a force exists?

In my experience, authentic people who "walk

their talk" are rare. Very few so-called "experts" are actually "the real deal."

I met Pat O'Connor several years ago when he was recommended to me by another respected colleague. I was looking to put a multimedia event together, and I reached out to him. From the beginning, I could tell the level of quality of this man and his organization. I could tell he had the respect of the people that worked for him, and he was special and rare. He did everything he said he would in the time that he said he would, and for a very fair price.

Again, I have been in practice and had businesses for over thirty years, and during that time I have come across few people who have truly impressed me with the quality of their work and their integrity. I can tell you that over the years, I have found quality of service, honesty, and integrity in business to be rarer now than ever before.

Over the years, because of our mutual respect, I came to know Pat O'Connor, and eventually I was proud to call him a friend. I met his incredible family and got to know his children. There was obvious love and respect for him from his wife and kids.

His daughter, who is also in the music industry, was roommates with my daughter, and they have become great friends. Pat's daughter would always speak of her father in a very loving and respectful way. Pat's daughter and son are as impressive as any young people I have met. Pat and his kids have helped my own daughter through her music career and have always been there without fail.

I have come to see Pat in a variety of scenarios. And in every way, he is one of the most impressive, intelligent, kind, and ethical people that I have ever met. If there was ever someone who is the "real deal" in every way, it is Pat. If there was ever anyone who has the moral high ground to give advice to others regarding success, it is Pat.

In this book, Pat puts in crystallized form his philosophies and experiences for others to learn from and follow. He condenses a life well-lived into seven basic rules that anyone can follow. Life is complicated. We all know that only the most thoughtful and knowledgeable visionaries can take something incredibly complex and explain it in clear, simplistic terms.

In *Getting It*, I also found refreshing the balance of authenticity, vulnerability, and credibility. So many authors attempt to artificially build themselves up by pretending to have never made a mistake, implying that they were always perfect, leading with credibility to show how great they are.

In my experience, people who claim to manifest perfection are not the real deal. Secure and authentic leaders speak freely about their mistakes and failures, often revealing their vulnerabilities in a way that is relatable to everyone.

In this book, Pat openly reveals countless mistakes, his regrets and missteps, and his frailties and failures. Rather than taking away from his credibility, Pat's openness adds to the credibility of his message.

I believe we all have a purpose in life, and I believe that to find that purpose, one must look at their own failures or challenges. No two lives are the same. We all face challenging times in our lives. Some find ways to overcome and use these times to become stronger and smarter, ultimately using their responses to challenges to achieve a level of success and happiness that they might not have found without facing challenges.

In this book, Pat recounts elements from his own life in a way that can help others to better understand how to overcome their own frailties and mistakes, and ultimately turn their lives around.

To me, this understanding is the true value of *Getting It*. As an author, Pat is both humble and powerful at the same time. But most of all, Pat is real. How do I know this? Recently, I had a personal health issue that I only shared with my family and close friends. I shared it with Pat because I knew he had overcome a couple of health challenges himself. Pat gave me some advice based on his own experience, and he said he would pray for me.

Since then, almost every day, Pat has sent me a message that he is thinking and praying for me. This has been happening now for more than a year. Virtually every day, without fail he texted me a message to let me know he was with me, and to give me strength. Most people can't do anything for themselves every day for thirty days much less for a year, and much less for someone else.

As of now, my health issue is virtually gone, and I credit that to many factors. But I think the biggest single factor, besides my wife and closest friend, was Pat. When he talks about the power of consistency in this book, Pat is talking about a practice that he lives on a daily basis.

I loved this book! I highly recommend this book to everyone and anyone searching for answers, for those going through a difficult time, or for anyone who just wants to get to the next level and be the best person they can be.

-Dr. Robert Melillo

Acknowledgements

I have always felt that we form our strongest relationships while in our highest states of emotional flux. Switching schools at the age of fourteen, I met the woman to whom I've now been happily married for the past thirty-eight years, the amazing men and women who would become my in-laws, and the Cardinal O'Hara High School and Steel Field guys with whom I would remain friends for life.

Striving to succeed in the music industry as an artist, I would form lifelong friendships with recording engineers, club owners, and musicians. Living in Houston, Texas for two years after graduating college, the bonds formed with my fellow apprehensive Texas transplants at the time would feel like the warmth one feels with family.

And the friends with whom I have collaborated—too many to name here, as the list could fill an entire book—and by whose grace and presence I've learned so much about the music industry, the sports world, the student activity sanctuaries at universities, the concert booking, promotion and production landscape, the corporate marketing world, and the spirit realm in which we all dwell.

These precious souls I've come to know and love as they have saved me from certain failure and provided a level of stability and emotional shelter to sustain me through so many unexpected storms along the way. These people have meant the world to me and have created the very oasis in which I live. These relationships have often been born of angst and trepidation, transitioning into a remedy for fear and uncertainty, and ultimately resulting in what can only be described as love.

It is to all of these loved ones; to my wife and kids, family members, my parents and sister, my in-laws, my friends, aunts, uncles, nieces, nephews, cousins, and so many of life's unexpected and uninvited—but much appreciated—angels in disguise that I dedicate this book.

If *Getting It* resonates with you, I hope it provides some useful ideas and assures you that you are not alone in this world. If it doesn't resonate with you, I hope it makes you laugh. And if you're searching, I hope it gives you some paths to consider.

I've always believed that if my last words to

anyone were anything other than "I love you," then I have screwed up. So, to all who have shown me kindness before I deserved it, wisdom before I could grasp it, and patience as I tried to learn and adjust, thank you, and please know that I love you.

And to those who gave up on me too soon, all is forgiven... see you on the other side.

Introduction

In the absence of love, any open arms will do. In the absence of vision, the lost wander. In the absence of hope, people despair. In the absence of courage, some let fear rule their lives.

Getting It is about finding what one loves most and then prioritizing all the things that matter. It's about managing fear, doubt, and indecision in a way that overrides the impulses to pass up what matters most in favor of what one desires in the moment.

Getting It is what often happens too late in life, if it happens at all. Perhaps ignorance is bliss, but failure is not. And after six decades of people-watching, I began to notice similar traits among those who seem to have it together. I also noticed common traits among those who do not.

Getting It is my attempt to crystalize the differences into seven simple rules. We all frame reality from where we see the world. I've been blessed with a childhood filled with love, an education focused on science and engineering, a professional career in the music industry, and an entrepreneurial journey surrounded and guided by friends, mentors, and some of the most entertaining characters one could hope to meet.

I hope *Getting It* shines a light on some areas of your life that could benefit from attention, and I hope that it inspires you to meet the challenges of life with enthusiasm, optimism, and a sense of certainty that you are right where you are for a reason.

Most of all, I hope *Getting It* serves as a reminder that regardless of your economic status, regardless of your family and circle of friends, and regardless of the influence you may or may not wield, you carry within you the seeds of greatness. You are far more powerful, more beautiful, and more loved than you will ever realize, and you have the capacity to move mountains if you choose to do so.

Thanks for checking out my book and for what you mean to more people than you may already be aware.

Table of Contents

Chapter 1: Why Bother?...1

Chapter 2: From "Oh God" To "Oh, God" 12

Chapter 3: Knock Twice 'Cause You Never Know 20

Chapter 4: Intelligent Life Out There 34

Chapter 5: Friends Make All The Difference 57

Chapter 6: Reframing Opportunity 69

Chapter 7: Tuning In On The Insanity Of Love 83

Chapter 8: Love And The Other Cheek 93

Chapter 9: Meeting The Challenge 110

Chapter 10: Love, Trouble, And The Space Between 128

Chapter 11: Boss Of Me 138

Chapter 12: Be Coming...147

Chapter 13: The Heart Of A Champion 160

Chapter 14: The Moment..169

Chapter 15: All Of The Lessons I'm Taught Until I'm Willing To Learn ...176

Chapter 16: Answering The Bell..185

Chapter 17: Seven Rules And The Spiritual Journey 191

Chapter 18: WTF... Why The Faith? 200

Chapter 1
Why Bother?

From time to time, I am invited to speak on university campuses about business, entrepreneurship, and the music industry. The lectures tend to be very informal, often with lengthy, animated Q&A sessions—some as long as three hours. I love the energy of the college kids and the optimism that accompanies many of these young and enthusiastic hearts.

I think many of these students see me as an example of how good things can happen to someone of average intelligence who works hard, and who has faith that such hard work will be rewarded.

During one Q&A, a student asked me how successful I was. It was an interesting question. I told him that it all depends on how you measure success; if he was asking about Net Financial Worth, I guess I was okay, but not all that successful.

If the units of measure consisted of degrees of happiness brought by being married to my best friend who happens to be the kindest person I've ever met, by being the dad to two amazing grown children, by having been blessed with the best parents, sister, and in-laws a man could hope for, by having long-standing friendships with people that I love like family—many of whom I've loved since high school, by enjoying good physical and mental health, by living in a nation that provides me with the opportunity to thrive, by making a living doing what I enjoy most, and by earning enough money to be comfortable and send my kids to great schools... then I suppose I've crushed it!

The amused student smilingly asked me, "well, how do you do that?" I told him it's a combination of being blessed, being grateful, staying in the moment, and living with intention. As the unofficial poster child for undiagnosed ADD, for me it's mostly about being blessed, but then we started talking about how to get blessed.

I told him that I believe life bestows upon all of us the opportunity to find the good in other people, to become close with some, and to stumble upon mentors. I told him about my Seven Rules, and the importance of writing out a description of and visualizing the life that you expect, including:

who you want to spend your life with, what kind of impact you'd like to have, how you can be the best in the world at something, and how to get up every time you get knocked down.

When he suggested I write a book, it occurred to me that he was the most recent in a string of students and business associates who had suggested the same thing.

The idea of writing a book felt a little pretentious. Who am I to write a book? But then again, with the peculiarly wide range of experience I've had since starting my business in 1990, with the eclectic group of mentors by whom I'm regularly influenced, and with my own desire to help people, who am I not to write a book? At a minimum, it might serve as a nice memento for my kids when I die. And at its best, it could change someone's life for the better.

So, what would I write about? How about the long road to getting it? So, I wrote it, and here it is.

Early in life, I came to understand three things: the Great Unknown loves me; I do not have God figured out—that's why I call Him/Her/It "The Great Unknown;" and I will never completely figure out The Great Unknown.

So, I guess that means I will not be able to figure Him/Her/It out for you, either. I'm not an evangelist. I'm more of a seeker who has tripped over several bumps in the road, despaired a few times, asked for help, and found it in the most unusual forms from some of the most unlikely people.

Getting It is based on my beliefs and experiences, and it is intended to present another perspective from which to view and engage with life. As a reflection of my own experiences, this book is intended to be respectful of other approaches as well—I have yet to meet the person who has the market cornered on wisdom. And when it comes to spiritual wisdom, please re-visit points #2 and #3 above; I do not have God all figured out, and I never will.

My influencers range from Harvard MBAs, rock stars, Fortune 500 executives, and ministers, to substance abusers, unhoused people, and blessed souls who have made some poor decisions when they didn't understand how precious they really were. I'm no more correct than anyone else, and when I stumble across a gem, I believe it's just something that's been left for me to share. Hopefully, you'll find a few gems in *Getting It*.

I begin this book not as a scholar, but rather as a student of success and of life itself. As I lament the times I've come up short, attempted to define a trail moving forward, and worked to have some kind of positive impact on this world, I have been repeatedly puzzled by how few people actually get it. I am comfortable making this statement because so often, I have found myself not getting it. Maybe I still don't, but I get more of it than I used to.

As a biophysics major at the University of Pennsylvania back in the 80s, I graduated without spending much time on campus. I was busy working hard, spending time studying, and getting the grades to graduate. I understood the importance of my relationships with someone I called God, with Dot (to whom I have now been married since 1984), with my family, and with my high school friends. These relationships, as well as those with my children, have been the foundation of my life.

Ironically, it never occurred to me that life is dynamic, and the zest with which I had pursued the first eighteen years of my life should have carried into college and full-time employment.

But it didn't. I quickly became interested in the trappings of success, rather than success itself. My training in school prepared me for this kind of fall, i.e., getting the grade has nothing to do with learning. Grades or accolades are just someone else's opinion of how I stack up against the competition, with both my performance and the competition being identified by someone else.

Such evaluations have little to do with objective reality. They are just the opinions of people whose jobs and careers were validated by the opinions of other people, who in turn were validated by those who came before them. It doesn't mean their intentions are wrong, nor does it mean they don't know more than I do.

However, they may be working from a different set of values on a competitive plane that may not apply to someone working in the creative realm where competition does not exist in its traditional form and such measurements do not apply.

My desire to appear successful in my early years manifested itself in working all the time—not necessarily producing anything, just working all the time. It resulted in me measuring myself against others. Sadly, there are only two ways to be Top Dog: you can be the best or you can convince yourself the others aren't so great either.

However, the love and relationship with something bigger than life was missing, perhaps a Creator, whose love for each of us would have nothing to do with our cars, our houses, our physique, or the bluster with which we present ourselves.

I think of "getting it" as one's willingness to accept responsibility for their life as an ever-changing process. It's not about a comparison with others, or our performance against some metrics developed by others. Getting it is about knowing that we are worth loving, choosing love when we feel fear, having and instilling faith in the people with whom we choose to engage, knowing what matters most, keeping the things that matter most at the forefront, not allowing room for the temptation to give in to what feels good now, replacing these desires with the things that matter most, and getting up every single time we are knocked down while believing in ourselves and the love that made us when every ounce of emotion tells us to stay down. Getting it matters. Getting it is the difference between existing and living.

Those who get it accept responsibility for results with little regard for effort. They stick to their values and accept the mission, understanding that they cannot control all parameters and having the courage to persevere anyway. In fact, I believe that those who truly get it typically enjoy the process, and they accept the obstacles as challenges that make the effort exciting. The pain of obstacles is temporary, but regret lasts forever. This permanence is why it's so important to know what matters most. It's different for everyone, but without that compass, activity can feel like progress, fun can feel like joy, and regret can become despair. That's how important it is to get it.

I don't believe that getting it has much to do with making money or becoming famous; although, I've seen these results in a lot of people who get it. To me, getting it has to do with a sense of balance that manifests itself in the ongoing development of one's mental, physical, emotional, spiritual, and relationship growth. Getting it is all about developing the habit of constant improvement, sharing it with others, and committing to raise the bar—not out of a sense of obligation, but rather from a desire to step up to the challenge.

Once I committed to understanding more about the mental dynamics of getting it, I was surprised to find out that people have been writing about the subject for thousands of years and many of their writings were similar to each other and to my own new-found approach. It is the spiritual basis of my philosophy that I believe makes it unique; I believe in positive thinking, I believe in conditioning the subconscious mind, I believe in goal setting, I believe in visualizing outcomes as if the desired outcome is already present in our lives, and I believe in developing the personal habits that produce effectiveness.

However, I believe the key to these tools and techniques working in my life hinges on my relationship with The Great Unknown... for short, let's call Him/Her/It "God" for now.

The Get / The Recap

Your level of success depends largely upon your definition of success. Since much of one's happiness is dependent upon how successful they believe they are, it's a good idea to define success in terms that serve you and inspire you to continue the journey.

The corollary to this first point is that one should ignore all thoughts that are not empowering. This is where meditation can be so valuable in honing the mind to hang on to the thoughts that help and to let go of the destructive thoughts.

A second corollary to this first point is that most criticism or sources of embarrassment are only as personal as we allow them to be. I once heard this expressed in a play on the phrase "mind over matter," with the twist being that if I don't mind, then your opinion does not matter. It's not important to tell someone their opinion doesn't matter, but once we have mined that value from a situation or from unsolicited feedback, there's nothing wrong with just letting any associated emotions go.

Every one of us is endowed with the capacity for greatness. "Who am I to write a book?" "Who are you to expect success and a fulfilling life?" Nobody has the right to tell us what we must believe, but I can say with certainty that if you choose to acknowledge that you are a child of God (or whatever you wish to call this entity), infused with divine DNA, then you will approach every challenge with a clear understanding of your capacity to win.

It's easy to confuse success with the trappings of success. Trappings and pleasure come and go, while real happiness lasts. Sadly, so does regret.

The race is not with everyone else; it is with

the best YOU that you can be. Maybe in the early phases of change, it's just between you and whomever you were before today. Life is easier when we root for everyone and write our own stories.

Accepting that the race is not with everyone else means making our own parade. When we make our own parade, we may find ourselves alone. That's okay; when we just keep moving with confidence, the crowd eventually catches up.

Getting off to a good start does not guarantee a successful race. Embrace the bumps in the road and keep driving that thing like you stole it.

Getting it requires taking responsibility, sticking to one's values, committing to constant improvement, and enjoying the process. Go ride that wave.

Chapter 2
From "Oh God" to "Oh, God"

On a plane trip to Los Angeles many years ago, I had the pleasure of being part of an emergency landing. I was traveling alone. Like most people in this position, my immediate thoughts centered on what my family would do if the plane actually crashed and burned, but I was distracted by the variety of responses I saw around me.

A woman and her husband, seated immediately to my left, were calmly holding hands—I believe they were praying. Another couple with the window and center seats to my right were totally losing it.

I was quietly asking God to take care of my children and wife, and I prayed that my parents would respond to my death by coming closer to God, rather than responding bitterly. We tend to get on a first-name basis with God when it feels like we're about to die.

Some people in the row in front of me seemed visibly shaken by the pilot's lack of discretion in leaving an open mic as he expressed his frustration with the plane's performance. I was a bit concerned, and in hindsight, I'm disappointed with my own failure to have complete faith and be at peace... but then again, how do you have unconditional faith in an entity you're calling "The Great Unknown?"

I was also a bit annoyed with the pilot who could have just as easily announced that our delay and multiple circles over LAX were due to traffic instead of uttering announcements that had no real meaning to most of us.

Anyway, an idea occurred to me as we made our final descent—one that felt much like a roller coaster ride. My thought was that if God is real, and if He/She/It truly loves each of us, then all things are as they should be, and this is the most exciting plane trip I've ever been on!

It's not very profound, but that simple thought made all the difference. I couldn't change the fact that we might crash, and I certainly was not in a position to help Captain Discretion land the jet. But by controlling my reaction to the situation, I would be prepared to do whatever was necessary when we reached the ground and possibly aid in calming some of the people around me during our descent.

While the landing was successful, and in fact, was probably more routine than many of us on the plane had feared, it was the kind of event that brings life's "real priorities" to light. Personally, I see life's priorities as significance, love, and the certainty of eternal peace, in ascending order. In this book, I would like to explore the relationship between these priorities and success in all aspects of life.

At the age of twelve, I felt lost and unloved. I was confused and didn't know why. Ironically, I was growing up in a house with very loving parents and a wonderful sister, I was doing well in school, and notwithstanding some self-control issues, I had always been a pretty good kid. However, like many young men, I was unable to understand the emotions that became obvious to me when I had a wife and children of my own.

What was missing was that relationship with something or someone who understood what I was feeling, saw my shortcomings, and knew that I would continue to struggle, but would love me anyway.

Fortunately for me, a young protestant seminarian named Paul Thompson—we called him

Moose—was running the youth ministry at a church across the street from my parents' house in the suburbs of Philadelphia. I had no interest in ministry, but I did enjoy basketball, and part of the church plan was to attract adolescents using sports as the bait and sneak in the message about God. All of us understood their little Trojan Horse game, and I took advantage of the basketball without paying much attention to their message... until one September afternoon in 1972.

I liked Moose and his fiancée Beth, and although I didn't feel like listening to preaching, I thought it would be impolite to say "no" when Moose asked to speak with me about faith. So, I listened while Moose read a couple Bible readings: John 3:16 and Romans 5:6. The gist was that God sacrificed his son who died for us knowing that we were sinners.

That afternoon, I gave my life to Christ with no real understanding of what I was doing, just a basic belief that any God willing to send his son to die for me, a gesture that means so much more to me now that I have children of my own, was worth committing to.

Ironically, life quickly became much more complicated. The funny thing about asking God into my life was that rather than solving all of my problems, it just illuminated—and essentially mocked—all of my problems instead. I behaved like a fool, got bullied, blamed everyone else for my own insecurities, finally realized the problem was me, asked for forgiveness from everyone, switched schools, started over, began playing the piano in studios, bars, and bands, found myself suddenly accepted for the stupidest of reasons (musical talent), parlayed it into a little vanity business, recorded two albums, and scraped by in college... Then came The Awakening!

Having been rejected three times on proposals of marriage to my then-girlfriend, now-wife, and having some concern over my ability to land the type of job I wanted in Philadelphia, I moved to Houston, Texas. My thought process was entirely wrong; I should not have needed to leave the fifth largest market in the country to find a job. Also, in leaving, I was doing something to my parents for which I would later have to bite my tongue when my own children chose to put their careers first and told me that my happiness was not their top priority. Karma is indeed a bitch. But my sojourn to Houston led to lessons that would stay with me for the rest of my life.

When I arrived in "Boomtown," as they called it in the 80s, I felt more alone than I had ever been; my family and friends were all in Philadelphia, and no one in Texas was impressed with—or even aware of—my musical ability. I had no credit, so I had to put down several months' front rent on my tiny, dirty, apartment, leaving me penniless, and an accounting error with my new company meant I wouldn't be paid for a couple of months.

Add to this a moving snag that delayed my furniture and the insect population indigenous to Texas, and I found myself very hungry, sleeping on the floor, and waking with roaches on me each morning. I was too desperate to see the light at the end of the tunnel, too stupid to admit to my parents that I had screwed up, and too proud to fix things right away.

It was on one of the loneliest nights of my life, barfing into a leaky toilet, cursing the only source I could turn to, that I realized I was not alone; nor would I ever be alone again. That September afternoon in 1972 came rushing back into my mind. I had bet on The Great Unknown, and that Great Unknown had never left me.

It was on this evening at the age of twenty-one that I finally realized the meaning of my decision at the age of twelve. I was, in fact, a child of God with the potential and the mandate to go do something with my life.

Once this truth became apparent to me, I began to see more to my past than had been obvious before. First, I noticed that each time I had wanted to change, it was never very difficult. The desire for change itself had always been enough to summon to my consciousness the required solutions. Even today, in spite of my most thoroughly developed strategies, a series of unplanned stumbles have resulted in most of my best decisions. And the confidence to fuel these decisions was based on the pivot from "Oh God!" to "Oh, God."

The Get / The Recap

When we control our reactions to what happens around us, we have the ability to control the game and our own nerves. Courage is the management of fear. It's less of a quality and more of a state that we create when we choose to do so. Courage is a form of control; when we control our reactions, we assume the quality of appearing to be courageous.

Relationships are valuable and worth maintaining. When everything is about to end, all that matters are our relationships and the love we've shared.

Every unplanned stumble brings with it the capacity to move toward what we want most. We are built to transcend tough times, and challenges remind us of our power if we allow ourselves to exercise courage.

Chapter 3
Knock Twice, 'Cause You Never Know

Back when I was a young musician in college, the complaint I always heard from fellow musicians was that it was "impossible" to get played on the radio. For the most part, this was true, with the exception of local shows. Fortunately for me, I didn't know how radio worked.

So, one night, the Wednesday before Thanksgiving in 1980, I went down to WMGK, Magic 102.9 in Philadelphia, with an album I had just recorded. The station, of course, was closed. But back then, security was not what it is now, so I followed an overnight employee onto an elevator to the correct floor and wandered around for a while, trying all the emergency exits to the station.

I finally found one that would open and walked around the hallway inside the station until I reached what I believed was the room where the DJ would be. And then I knocked... and knocked... and knocked again, to no avail. But eventually, everyone has to take a leak, and this DJ was no exception. To my delight, it was Tom Richards, a voice I had often heard on the radio but with whom I had never connected a face.

Tom put a song on and had three and a half minutes to take care of business. When he came back, he gave me a quick stare up and down with a look that said, "Who the hell are you, and what the hell are you doing here?" Fortunately, Tom was the kind of guy who understood what I was trying to do, probably respected the effort, and was too nice of a guy to send me back out into the cold. That night was the start of a friendship and musical kinship that has lasted more than forty years.

In addition to teaching me about the radio business and introducing me to every song that every person should study during their lifetime, Tom became my guitarist, bassist, musical muse, and one of my best friends. Over the course of several decades, Tom and I have jammed, talked, and schemed our way through a multitude of labyrinths. It was Tom that would encourage me when I needed it, push me when I was getting lazy, and stay up all hours of the night while we created music and took a shot at the title.

One of the songs on which Tom played bass and guitar was called "Harbor Light." It was a song I wrote with Amy Grant in mind. I was convinced that if I could get the song into Amy's hands, she would record it, and everything would take off from there.

So I did what any dedicated artist would do: on October 9, 1991, I went to an Amy Grant concert at the Spectrum in Philly, sent a Philadelphia Fun Pack filled with Flyers jerseys and Eagles stuff for her kids, snuck backstage, got chased by security, bumped into a relative of her drummer with whom I had done some recording sessions, grabbed a backstage pass that kept me from being arrested, found out from her guitarist where she and the band were staying, drove to the Park Hyatt Hotel, tracked them down to a rooftop lounge, gave my credit card to the bartender (it was a safe move; Contemporary Christian bands generally don't run up much of a bar tab!), crashed the band get-together, and ended up sitting at a grand piano singing "Harbor Light" for Amy.

The song never did make it into Amy's repertoire, but something happened that night that was life-changing for me. There is absolutely no way that I should have been able to end up sitting at a piano in a room with Amy Grant. Somehow, the combination of my persistence, Amy's kindness, and some kind of divine intervention brought about results that were pretty ridiculous. It changed my definition of "impossible." The state of "impossible" is just in our minds; there is actually no such thing as "impossible."

Ironically, my own recording of the song did end up winning me the 1991 BMI Best New Songwriter Award, which in turn introduced me to several talented recording artists, musicians, songwriters, Philadelphia on-air radio personality Cyndy Drue (who started playing me on the radio), and a young Mark Fried who managed writer-publisher relations at BMI, the performing rights organization.

Starting with that amazing evening at the Spectrum in Philadelphia—and some wonderful hangs in NYC with Mark Fried (who went on to start Spirit Music and eventually Mojo Music)—I suddenly found myself in the music business. Until then, I had felt like an outsider, slogging it out in bars, begging for studio session gigs, independently releasing my own music at a time when there were no viable distribution or promotional channels for such endeavors, looking in and wishing someone would open the door. Finally, I was in.

Interestingly enough, "in" can take on many meanings. I thought it would mean a career as a musician... but such careers are meant for far more talented guys than I, with better chops, better looks, and much more swagger. What "in" did mean was that I would be poised to make a play when the opportunity presented itself.

That opportunity did present itself in the spring of 1994. I was at a Philadelphia Flyers hockey game back when you could walk right up to team owners... this was all pre-9/11 when security was not really an industry of its own. So, I had a chance encounter with Mr. Ed Snider, builder of the Spectrum, owner of the Flyers, founder of Spectacor, and eventual chairman of Comcast Spectacor. I suggested to Mr. Snider that if the Flyers would send me footage, I could leverage some of my new entertainment industry relationships to edit music videos with the hockey highlights for the Spectrum's new video scoreboard.

Mr. Snider said "yes," and within months (thanks to Mr. Snider, Mark Piazza, Mark Di-

Nardo, the Flyers, the NHL's Glenn Adamo, Patti Fallick, Adam Acone, Ward Glassmeyer, Jon Litner, and League Commissioner Mr. Gary Bettman) I was doing the same for every arena in the NHL as well as for NHL Productions.

Before long, Tom Grabowski and then Jill D'Alessandro and Jay Abraham at NASCAR's production facilities, followed by Melissa Verille, Keith D'Alessandro, Tally Hair, Steve Stum, Phil Metz, and Amanda Oliver at NASCAR, and shortly thereafter, Christine Reimel at NFL Films, began providing me—and therefore POC Media—with opportunities to support their music supervision efforts.

My two takeaways were that first, it requires a lot of people to approve an idea when you are dealing with a large entity like a major sports organization, and second, my original business model had me doing everything for free. It would be up to me to figure out how to get paid. Coming up with a great idea is useful, executing on that idea separates one from the pack, figuring out how to monetize the execution of a great idea is the stuff that sleepless nights are often made of, and crafting a working model ends up being much more challenging than expected.

My best shot at creating a revenue stream and business model felt like the NHL, as I was in a position to control the entire product; POC Media was actually editing the videos with the blessings of the NHL and record labels, as opposed to just creating awareness for music discovery and licensing as we were doing at the NFL and NASCAR production facilities.

After pitching several brands on sponsoring our NHL In-Arena Videos, I realized that between NHL league sponsors and individual team sponsors, I was competing with better equipped salespeople who could package brand activations with their advertising and signage. This allowed them to carve out brand-exclusivity categories. In other words, brands weren't going to buy into my scoreboard video packages when they could get better deals from teams and the league.

Next, I pitched labels, and they all turned me down—twice. After two rounds of label rejections, I got lucky on the third version of the pitch. Bruce Kirkland, the CEO of EMI-Capitol Entertainment Properties (LA), Madelyn Scarpula from Mercury (NYC), Kim Markovchick of Mercury (Nashville), and Kate Tews and Cynthia Sexton of Virgin Records (LA) agreed to take a chance and work with me. At that time, unbeknownst to any of these people, having drained the equity in our home to purchase the video equipment needed to deliver for the NHL, I was within weeks of going under. They literally saved my business and my home! Needless to say, I LOVE Bruce, Madelyn, Kim, Kate, and Cynthia!

There was soon a cavalcade of supporters, too long to list here (see the appendix for the rest of the list), who gave me the opportunity to make a living doing what I enjoyed for the next several decades. Within five years of being turned down by every major music company at least twice, we were now working for almost every label in New York, L.A., and Nashville. Each person I've listed above and in the appendix played some role in allowing me to pursue my dreams. We were off to the races! I thought there would be no looking back!

When Charlie Rosenzweig of NBA Entertainment allowed us to present N.E.R.D. featuring a young Pharrell Williams for some NBA Finals promo spots on NBC, we suddenly began to get major attention with prime-time commercial visibility. Before long, POC Media was producing commercials for championship apparel associated with the NHL, NBA, and MLB. Thanks to Susan Moss of NASCAR, we even shot, scored, edited, and produced four broadcast institutional commercials for NASCAR on ESPN.

By the mid-90s, record labels were throwing money at exposure as the sale of high-margin compact discs (CDs) had already reinvigorated the music catalog business in the 80s. People were re-purchasing their favorite albums on CD by the late-80s and the trend was at an all-time high in the 90s. There were four sports broadcast networks (NBC, ABC, CBS, and FOX), one cable sports network (ESPN), and approximately ninety arenas and stadiums between the NFL, NBA, NHL, and MLB. We were ready to move into all of them with our promotion of music to sports venues and broadcasters. The future looked amazing!

But every game has its ebbs and flows, the score changes, and even the best teams need to adjust. iTunes took the record business from a high-margin album and CD business to a much lower-margin singles and download business, while digital streaming platforms brought the value of a music release down even further. A new proliferation of cable channels presented more broadcast sync opportunities, but the profits of premium seating sections and suites led to the construction of new stadiums and arenas, now with self-contained studios to house the expanding universe of cable networks. All of this limited our value to both the record labels and the teams for a while.

It became clear that POC Media's business model would need to change. Luckily, I had hired a diverse group of people who were willing to work hard and were able to change direction on a moment's notice. A twenty-two-year-young Kristi Kopach (now Kristi Crocker) managed many of the record label relationships for my company, while Mike Danese and Ray Collins shared the helm running production. Ira Rosenzweig, Jeff Preston, Rich Capello, and Marc Giordano produced innovative multimedia, and Steve Graham took care of the corporate marketing clients. In the meantime, we re-tooled and prepared to re-launch new models for the entertainment industry.

When you need to get the door open, sometimes you have to knock twice; sometimes you have to hit the wall over and over until it falls down. In my case, survival would mean getting teams and sports organizations to help me be the liaison between their sponsors and the music industry: creating experiential marketing opportunities, producing branded concerts, and finding creative ways to write checks back to the record labels from sponsoring brands. Eventually, it meant challenging a young Andrew Roomberg to get more creative than ever with coding processes that were still in their developmental phases.

It required laying out a vision for our clients and team-members and working with a small POC Media team that included Andrew, my wife, my son Christian, his bass player, Christian Orellana, the aforementioned Tom Richards, and anyone else who was willing to help. We needed to automate our in-house music clearance process in a way that could provide value for sports broadcasters, leveraging that technology for venues, and associating brands with our initiatives to fund artist development in a mutually beneficial way. This was a chance to crash and burn, or a shot at the title; and at that time, I wasn't sure which path I was looking at.

Ultimately, creativity and persistence won out. But it took years, many sleepless nights, some challenges to my faith, and a lot of financial and emotional sacrifices on the part of my family.

Eventually, POC Media was able to launch initiatives that created "win-win-win-win-win" value for brands, broadcasters, sports teams, retail outlets, and record labels. Non-disclosure agreements prevent me from publicly acknowledging the sports broadcast producers and music supervisors who were willing to take a chance on POC Media, but they are all well aware of my gratitude, and they have all been vital to the success of both my businesses and my family.

After a series of experiential marketing platforms that ranged from branded concerts to consumer retail activations, POC Media finally struck gold by developing the first-ever music licensing and curation system to leverage both artificial intelligence and blockchain technology, providing high-speed licensing and music discovery at a level never approached prior to our introduction of the platform.

Winning is rarely easy, and it's almost never a one-step process. Winning requires thinking things through, considering the obstacles down the road that one has yet to imagine, getting up every time one is knocked down, having faith that somehow things will work out; and then leveraging relationships and persistence to reach the desired goal. Sometimes winning is about knocking twice, or even a hundred times, because you never know what may happen!

The Get / The Recap

"Impossible" is just a word. It's a state of mind that can be overcome with faith and persistence.

Large organizations require more people to make simple decisions than smaller organizations, but they also provide higher critical mass, which can open many doors.

One must stay in the fight until one wins. Sometimes that means having your music or message heard, sometimes it means finding a new audience for what you're selling, sometimes it means going back to the same companies that have already said "no," and delivering a recrafted pitch.

Every game has its ebbs and flows. They don't give the Stanley Cup to the team that is ahead in the first period, unless they keep that lead through the third period and do it sixteen times, winning every series. When things change, we adjust. New information is neither good news nor bad news… it's just reality… it's just news.

Faith in one's team, in one's dreams, in oneself, in the notion that everything is going to be okay, is often the only way to get up after being knocked down. It also helps to believe that even when things are not necessarily okay, generally, life is still good. Even when I am having trouble finding the good, it still helps me to believe that I will eventually look back and understand the blessings that may not be obvious in the moment.

Chapter 4
Intelligent Life Out There

Persistence and confidence go a long way. Look at most of history's success stories and you'll find people who believed in what they were doing and knew that if they didn't give up, they would get what they wanted.

Thomas Edison tried thousands of different approaches to create a working light bulb, and he referred to the so-called failures as successes in singling out strategies that would not work. Marconi persisted in developing the radio in spite of many critics who called into question his mental stability.

The U.S. Patent Office published a statement in 1893 saying there was nothing left to be invented. Fortunately, people like Jonas Salk, Henry Ford, and Alexander Graham Bell had more confidence in their own ideas than in the opinions of the U.S. Patent Office, and these guys were willing to persist.

So, here's my big question: Why? Clearly,

these guys weren't foolish, yet they were willing to continue their pursuit of long shots despite the warnings presented by conventional wisdom. And they didn't pursue their dreams in a half-hearted way. Marconi's so-called friends had him committed for psychological evaluation when he announced that he could send audio signals from a transmitter to a receiver, sans wires. That didn't discourage Marconi. Nor did more than ten thousand failures discourage Edison from developing the light bulb.

In studying the lives of those who beat the odds, I have found two common threads: faith and certainty. But it wasn't until recently that the purpose of this faith and certainty revealed itself to me. Interestingly, it wasn't until later in life, through the prism of hindsight, that the significance of my own University of Pennsylvania education became clear to me.

When I graduated high school, I wasn't sure what to do with my life. I thought it would be fun to be a rock star—but I never really had the commitment, probably didn't have the talent, and certainly didn't have the looks or swagger to make it happen. I enjoyed math and science, believing that a career in science might be in the cards. But the continuing education requirements and lack of clear earning potential caused me to hedge my bets.

Giving in to the self-induced pressure to make the decision that would be most respected by those interested in my future, I decided to become a doctor—with no real faith or certainty that I had the mental or emotional capacity to pull it off. Indeed, my gut was correct, and by the time I was a sophomore, I had begun a core curriculum in chemical engineering as a hedge against changing my mind on the MD pursuit.

Following college, I began a career in industrial sales, peddling process control equipment in Texas, which led to success in marketing with a process level control company, and eventually, I secured a marketing position working for Honeywell.

The success I had in the corporate world masked the failure to get a record deal, the change of course from my medical pursuits, and the sense that I was playing it safe, when in fact, I was setting myself up for a major mid-life crisis.

After a few years of marriage, my wife conceived our first child, a wonderful little boy named Christian. Due to the unfair standard to which so many women must hold themselves, my wife felt strongly that she needed to continue her career as an audit manager at Arthur Andersen. Not because she loved the job, but because she didn't want to let down so many of the women she believed she was representing as a female achiever in a male-dominated world.

The unfair standard for women is the notion that in order to be a successful woman, one must make money, be pleasant at all times, be the perfect lover, be the perfect mother, be the perfect homemaker, be the world's best cook, and always look great doing it all. To this day, I still believe my wife makes the cut in all of these areas, although she has never seen herself through my eyes.

Fortunately, traditional success as a man only requires that one makes a lot of money, loves his wife and kids, and is faithful to the marriage. The first was a challenge; the last two came naturally.

In an effort to fulfill both of our goals, I decided, with my wife's blessings, to become Mr. Mom, and stay at home to raise Christian while getting my own business started. The experience was rewarding, developing a bond few fathers have with their sons. I also managed to get a small consulting and audio production business off the ground, although I continually sabotaged myself by cutting back whenever things got shaky.

It seemed that whenever I anticipated potential problems, problems arrived, and while I had developed relationships with many major sports organizations, record labels, and Fortune 500 companies, I soon found myself looking for the security of a job with a steady paycheck.

By the time Dot was six months pregnant with our second child—a beautiful little girl named Devon—I had begun a new stint as the Director of New Business Development with a marketing communications company. Shortly after Devon's birth, it became clear both to my new boss and to me that this job was not in my or the new company's best interest. Within four months, I was once again going into business for myself.

There was one major difference in my return to entrepreneurship as opposed to my first five-year stint. Having been embarrassed and disappointed with the results of my brief period of employment, I had decided that nothing short of the will of God would keep me from succeeding. That was when it seemed the future would open up.

Within four years, we were providing non-traditional channels of promotion for virtually every major record label, providing arena and stadium premium seating pitches for several major sports teams, producing broadcast and cable television segments that aired nationally, and creating integrated marketing strategies for the largest companies in the northeastern United States.

Business was suddenly booming, but rather than facing challenges with gusto, I was still nervous about whether the success would continue, and for decades, my business would approach that break-through point only to fall back harder than ever.

At the age of forty-one, when everything was looking great, my wife and I bought a big house on The Main Line (a nice suburb of Philadelphia). I bulked up on great employees, borrowed money to grow the business, and even trusted a couple of new employees to roam on their own and help grow my company.

Then, about a month later, a couple of planes flew into New York's World Trade Center, and everything changed. I should have just laid everyone off right away, but in an effort to be compassionate—and probably in a sense of not letting the terrorists win—I decided to keep all my employees and ran up a lot of debt as my monthly expenses were not being offset by business revenue.

This should be a lesson to young entrepreneurs: sometimes when you lose a round, it's better to take Kenny Rogers' advice about "knowing when to fold 'em." A couple of hiring mistakes, a big borrowing mistake, and a refusal to make the tough decision to lay people off cost me almost a decade of happiness, messed up my marriage, affected my health, crushed my faith, and probably caused me to put too much pressure on my own kids not to make the same mistakes I had made... Yep, my forties sucked!

By the age of forty-seven, I was more than one million dollars in debt. My wife, while always loving and supportive, had completely lost confidence that we would ever get back to zero, and those closest to me would constantly reassure me that I had touched a lot of people in a "special way," even if I had never made a lot of money.

I felt like a failure in front of my wife and kids, and after years of hard work, I had nothing to show for it; in fact, I had one million dollars less than nothing to show for it. My dad had joked that my biggest success was getting people to lend me enough money to be able to lose a million dollars.

My dad rarely pulled punches, and his insight was not meant as a compliment. Why I ever cared what he or anyone else thought is so far beyond me now, but for some reason, while I could generally ignore the peanut gallery, my dad's opinion mattered to me.

Ironically, through the filter of time, I can now see that the last thing my dad wanted was for me to care what he thought. Today, I realize that in his own way, he was trying to encourage me to ignore insults and move forward. They say that heaven has many mansions; apparently, so does love.

On February 6, 2008, I experienced one of the best nights of my life. Having written a song that would be used as a NASCAR Truck Race opening theme with Brad Arnold and Chris Henderson of the rock group 3 Doors Down, I felt legit. I was writing music with real rock stars, and they were treating me like a peer. It was a little late to call my parents and let them know about my evening, so I'd call in the morning.

Maybe I should have just woken them up with a call that night. On February 7, 2008, I hit my all-time low in Franklin, TN. Sleeping at the home of friends I was staying with on a business trip, partially because I love them and largely because I couldn't afford to keep renting hotel rooms, I was awakened by my cell phone.

The voice on the other end was the cracking, choked-up voice of my wife, Dot, as she told me that my dad had just been rushed to the hospital. Within ten minutes, I was booked on a flight home. My friends Allan and Shauna Hardin paid for the ticket, because they're kind, and I suspect they also knew I was broke and couldn't afford a same-day flight back to Philly. Within fifteen minutes, the second call had come to let me know that my dad had died.

My dad was always my biggest fan and generally my loudest critic. There was nothing in the world I wanted more than to succeed and hear my dad say, "Pat, way to go." And while I'm sure my dad was proud of me for who I was, on February 7th, 2008, I realized that I had failed to deliver for my dad. No matter what happened from that day forward, I would live with the fact that my father died without ever seeing me at my best.

As stupid and sexist as this sounds, I firmly believe that every man goes through life yearning to hit one or more out of the park in front of his father. As I mentioned to a friend after having given the eulogy at my dad's funeral, I'm sure that when the great Archie Manning passes on, both Peyton and Eli will be wishing they had each won a third Super Bowl for him.

For several months after my dad died, my life was a mess. I'm not sure if it was obvious to those on the outside, but I was really screwed up; did I mention earlier that my forties sucked? I failed to return phone calls, became bitter with God, lost my sense of compassion for others, and while I never publicly acknowledged it, I had inwardly returned to blaming everything and everyone else for my problems.

Luckily, a good friend joined me for lunch while I was on a business trip to Charlotte, North Carolina, and she shared one simple sentence that helped me pivot. She said, "Hey Pat, why don't you stop cursing your circumstances and start counting your blessings?" Now that's a good friend, someone who cares enough to help, who understands that it's not the right time to call you out on all of your bad behavior and whining, and just tells you to stop doing this and start doing that.

One of the results of counting one's blessings is that it sets one up to see the future with a sense of gratitude. How can one engage life with gratitude and not approach life with a positive attitude? If my dad was unimpressed with how I managed my business, he must have been laughing from the other side while watching how poorly I handled adversity and his passing.

Now, more than fifteen years removed from his death, I keep a picture of my dad on my home office bookcase. It's a great photo that he gave to everyone in our family as a joke one Christmas. It was taken as a business portrait at the engineering company where he worked. He's in his fifties, wearing a suit, looking into the camera with a subtle smile, almost a smirk. When things are going well with my business, I look up at that picture and it feels like he's smiling down upon me. When things are going poorly, it looks like he's about to laugh at me, making fun of me. I'm not sure if he's mocking my incompetence or my getting stuck in the moments and taking life so seriously, but it's a classic "Dad face." It's just a picture, but sometimes it feels like Dad's still hanging with us. I'm sure that if there are bleachers in Heaven, he's sitting there, watching the game, and rooting for me with a sense of certainty that I'll win.

CERTAINTY... Eastern philosophers apply it

to manifestation, religions use certainty as a foundation, and in life, it can be the difference between winning and losing. Certainty is one of the hardest things to sell but one of the easiest decisions to make. I don't remember where I first heard it, but I've heard it several times over the years. "What would you do if you had absolute certainty regarding the outcome?" Everybody has an answer, but very few have the courage to believe, with real faith, in themselves or their outcomes.

Luckily for me, at a time when the business challenges were mounting up and it was not apparent that I would ever get over the hump, I began seriously considering ending my own life... so finding the courage to believe was no longer an issue.

Now, to be clear, I am not advocating suicide. I think it's the biggest and most tragic mistake a person can make. And while we can only have compassion for anyone who feels desperate enough to give up, I believe that suicide is also the most selfish and cowardly decision a person can make, and only on the other side will such a troubled soul understand the ripple effect of the damage they've done. That said, I understand the dilemma.

Now here's the upside to suicidal thoughts: When you've come face to face with eternity, and you've decided that anything is better than life as you know it, you've arrived at a very empowering place. You can now stop taking life's punches and start hitting back. Nothing is more dangerous than someone on a mission with nothing to lose.

At a point when I was contemplating the most selfish and cowardly decision I could possibly make, love stepped up in the most unlikely form. In a week, when for a couple of evenings I was literally sleeping in my car in the parking lot of a Travel Lodge in El Segundo, California because I was out of money with no working credit cards, I made the brilliant decision to reach out for help. I was afraid, and I chose to share my fears with my most brutally honest, not-particularly-spiritual, brightest, and most unapologetically direct and pragmatic mentor, The Late and Truly Great, Bud Prager.

Prior to landing me two quick new clients and after listening through my whining meanderings once—which was something Bud taught me about analyzing a problem: listen once, and then move on to the solution—Bud spoke to me with the most peculiar but accurate take on biblical history that I've ever heard.

Bud said, "Patrick, meeting Goliath is what lifted a shepherd named David and gave him the opportunity to become king. Our opportunities often come disguised as terrifying behemoths. When you are face-to-face with your demons, it's time to grow some balls, slay that giant, take the crown, and become the king you were created to be!"

I don't think Bud dedicated much time to biblical study, but if God has the sense of humor that I believe only The Great Unknown can have, my friend Bud is standing next to Peter, arms folded, acting as the bouncer at the pearly gates, and running many of the operations on the inside as well. I suspect his mansion is quite opulent, and I can't wait to share another meal with him when I can finally see him again on the other side. Other than my own parents, there is no one that I miss more in life than Bud. Every contender needs a mentor, and Bud Prager was the best there will ever be.

For me, my failures had presented me with a choice: I could either cement my place in history as the coward that gave up when the going got a little shaky, or I could get back in the fight. The fact that I'm writing this book indicates that I opted for the latter.

Part of the commitment to stay in the fight meant making an effort to stay centered; spiritually, emotionally, physically, and relationally. For me, this involved getting up early, meditating, walking for an hour, and attending mass each day for a while, sometimes as early as 6:30 a.m. when it was just me and a couple of nuns at church. It wasn't that I thought mass helped me spiritually. It was more about pushing myself to never again find myself wondering if I had left any gas in the tank by the end of the race.

Frequently, while walking in the early morning, often as early as 4:30 a.m. before the sun rose, I would feel an intense level of energy, almost like goose bumps, surrounding me as I walked. At times, it felt as if the lighting outside was changing as I walked. Given the title of this chapter, I should hasten to say I was not experiencing UFO phenomena.

But there is indeed something out there: energy, a field of possibilities, something that feels like love, something that feels like faith. But faith can take two forms. When it's positive and constructive, faith inspires and takes those who share it to new heights. When it's negative, faith manifests itself in worry, fear, insecurity, anger, and illness.

Here's the rub: everyone has abundant faith; the only question is whether that faith is positive or negative. Unfortunately, it's easier to have negative faith; there are so many people and outlets to support it. If you have negative faith and you're wrong, no one will fault you, but if you have positive faith and things don't develop as hoped, look out!

That's why so many of us are told by our loved ones, "Don't get your hopes up, don't discuss your dreams with others, be realistic." My question is "WHY?" If something is important to you, does convincing yourself that it shouldn't be important and lying to your loved ones about what you really want make failure more palatable? And if it does, what does that say about how badly you really wanted it in the first place?

I was fortunate to learn at an early age that nothing I do will please everyone. In fact, it is absolutely impossible to please some people, and trying to do so will only lead to hurt feelings and a failure to pursue your dreams. So, given the need to be polite with and understanding of those who would like to help with your decisions, once you've decided to stop worrying about the well-intentioned opinions of others—many of whom don't have enough knowledge about your specific situation to offer a useful opinion anyway—how do you manifest results in your life, and where do the miracles come from?

I guess they come from that Great Unknown, and I always ask for God's help. My formal education and life experiences have led me to believe that The Great Unknown provides us with more influence over the field of possibilities than most people realize. What follows is a very incomplete summary of extensive research performed by some of the founders of quantum physics, including Niels Bohr, Werner Heisenberg, and Erwin Schrodinger. All three of these pioneers dealt with probability and explored both the wave and particle nature of energy.

To understand the meaning of wave functionality, picture a boat in the ocean. When a wave moves past the boat, the boat and water rise, and then fall back to their original positions. It is not the water particles that are moving across the ocean, but rather the wave. On the other hand, when a wave reaches the shore, it collapses, and the water particles rush to the beach. It is now the water particles, and not the waves, that are moving.

You may remember a school physics class when you shined a light through a ripple-tank, watching the waves interact, reinforcing and canceling each other. You were watching wave functionality in action.

This same wave functionality takes place in matter, specifically in the sub-atomic realm of protons, neutrons, and electrons. You may remember a high school science class when you first heard the expression $E=MC^2$. This was Einstein's formula for energy, and it states that energy is equal to an object's mass times the speed of light squared. A corollary of the formula states that neither matter nor energy can be created or destroyed, but rather, they change form. Without contradicting postulations surrounding such scientific frontiers as cold fusion or faster-than-light travel through the theorized space-time continuum, it seems safe to say that energy is a function of mass and speed.

The pioneers of quantum physics believed that an electron, once measured, was a particle; but until measured, it behaved as a wave. Erwin Schrodinger even developed an equation that calculates the probability of finding an electron at a given location, and he hypothesized that at any given time, the electron is part wave and part particle.

Here's a funny little related aside: I failed Organic Chemistry in college, leading to an encore performance in higher education that the University of Pennsylvania likes to call "Summer School." The course that I had to take was actually a Physical Chemistry (P-Chem) class to make room on my next semester schedule for my command re-performance in Organic Chemistry. Not realizing that my P-Chem final was an open book test, I showed up unarmed and had to derive the Schrodinger Equation from scratch.

It took me the whole two hours, so I didn't have time to answer the questions on the test. When time ran out, I just wrote on the Blue Book "Hey, I just derived the Schrodinger Equation!" My professor was so impressed that he gave me an "A" with the caveat that while my derivation bordered on genius, my failure to bring books to an open-book final bordered on some form of mental deficiency. That was one of the few "A"s that I landed in my entire college career, and the one I'm still most proud of. An important lesson on what to do when you get baffled: just answer the question you were hoping they would ask!

Okay, back to the wave-particle theory. If you are not a fan of science, by now you may be saying, "So What?!" But here is the significance of wave functionality, Schrodinger, Bohr, Heisenberg, and all of that stuff I just mentioned. Our brains create waves. These waves broadcast our intentions to The Great Unknown, to the universe, to other brains. These waves are both sent and received by each of us, and they can be collapsed by each of us in ways that increase the probability of positive answers to our prayers. And what is it that determines the way in which a wave form collapses? FAITH.

Skeptical? Have you ever been in a zone where everything you did worked? Perhaps you've seen athletes who are playing at their peak, or perhaps you've been in meetings where you could mysteriously anticipate what the other person was about to say. Perhaps you've felt the unmistakable guidance of God and wondered how that happened. While you have probably never thought it had anything to do with atoms and wave forms, is it possible that your faith—the broadcasting of your thoughts and intentions—created a form of energy that helped your cause?

There have been experiments on the healing power of prayer, some where the subjects were not aware that people were praying for them, and the prayers had a positive effect! There are people who can "light up a room" with the energy they share, and others who can do so by leaving. These feelings are all about "vibes" or vibrations. They're about vibrations we create through our thoughts.

If you golf, perhaps you can imagine lining up a four-foot putt that you should make. I would miss because I'm terrible at golf, but let's assume you actually play the sport. Would betting three thousand dollars on the putt increase or decrease your chances of making the putt?

If you don't have three thousand dollars, and the guy you just bet appears to be mean, the bet might adversely affect your putting. If you believe you will make the putt and are looking forward to buying a new set of clubs with the three thousand dollars, and assuming you can afford to pay the bet if you miss, the bet will probably help you to make the putt.

Your projected fear or passion, your focused intentions, and the prevailing thought on which you dwell will probably determine whether you make the putt.

The same is true of any person or organization trying to achieve a goal. Faith is more than just positive thinking; faith is positive knowing, and this knowing produces a form of energy that reaches God, the Universe, the Infinite Field of Possibilities, whatever you choose to call it. I call it God, because I believe that it's more than just a field of infinite correlations that loves us. Again, I do not have God figured out, so all respect to those who do not share my belief. I simply encourage anyone I meet to reach out to God. And if you feel like you know God is reaching back, this knowing is faith.

The Get / The Recap

Persistence is a MUST. If it matters, then you must stay in the fight.

What matters most is really all that matters. Second-best alternatives are just cheaper forms of something better, but they're not really better, they just appear that way to people who are looking for a fast solution or an escape from emotional pain.

GETTING IT

When the peanut gallery has given up on you, just ignore them and plan your comeback. In the paraphrased words of St. Teresa of Calcutta, it was never between you and them.

When it comes to worrying about what others think, consider the possibility that you don't even know what others think or what parameters are affecting their opinions. Maybe all of the people we think are watching us are actually busy with their own lives.

Some days actually do suck. Get over it and count your blessings.

Certainty matters. Winners find a way to believe, even if they're fooling themselves. Find a reason to believe.

Hope is believing that God can, while Faith is knowing that God will. Self-empowerment is having Faith when others only have Hope.

Sometimes our best opportunities show up disguised as giants. Manage the fear and slay those giants because you can. You were born for this moment, and you will carry the victory with you for life, or you will take your fear to your grave. What you believe matters. Have positive faith.

Chapter 5
Friends Make All the Difference

In the acknowledgements of this book, I touched on my belief that we form our strongest relationships while in our highest states of emotional flux. Back when I had a real job, there was an English woman with whom I worked; she had a great sense of humor and she spoke about things from time to time back in the UK. From some of her stories, I gathered that she must have been born in London around the early-to-mid-1930s.

One day, it occurred to me that she must have been a child during "The Blitz," when Germany spent nine months unmercifully bombing London during World War II. I inquired as to whether she would be offended at my asking her what it was like.

I expected to hear about horrific scenes of terror, but she floored me by saying they were the best times in her life and that she never felt more alive, more included, or more loved than during those bombing raids. She pointed out that during the raids, everyone bonded together... sure, they were afraid, but more than that, they were together, sharing the emotions and bonding together.

I don't expect to ever face anything remotely resembling what she and her family had to deal with, but her words stay with me to this day, and they provide a useful prism through which to observe the past and by which to approach the future.

Emotional flux is generally not fun, but the outcome can be amazing, and when we approach challenges with the sense that somehow the outcome will be amazing—even if we cannot yet grasp what that outcome will be—we can steer the outcome in a direction that serves us. For this reason, I adopted the belief long ago that most news is just news, neither good nor bad, it's just the starting point from which we find ourselves launching into the future. I also refuse to accept emotions into my life that do not empower me to face the future with optimism. It's not because some emotions are not justifiable; they are, but some emotions are also useless to anyone interested in having a happy life.

As a young child, I exhibited what teachers referred to as "behavioral issues." Ironically, I thought my teachers had behavioral issues. They were getting paid to teach, but they could only teach when circumstances perfectly suited their desires. Isn't that what I was getting in trouble for: my inability to learn when circumstances did not match my desires? Are you kidding me? I was just a young boy, I wasn't getting paid, and those who were getting paid wanted a nine-year-old to make their job easier! When I was a kid, teachers who cared seemed like an endangered species.

Eventually, I was lucky enough to stumble across some genuine teachers who wanted to enable young kids to unlock their potential. My ninth-grade science teacher, Mr. Brockman, once took me aside and suggested that I tailor my jokes away from making fun of others and let myself be the brunt of my jokes. He also suggested that I look for ways to help other kids who might feel self-conscious in school, or who might not be as prepared as they needed to be.

That advice was life-changing; until that conversation, I had never noticed that my biting sense of humor had the potential to hurt other people. I had also assumed that we all see life from an even playing field. With a few kind words, Mr. Brockman helped me understand that my ninth-grade perception could not have been further from reality.

My ninth-grade English teacher, Mr. Silvestri, used to give us daily quizzes, which counted heavily toward our grades. His point was that in life, everything counts. He was correct. Every second counts, and we never know which ones will bring blessings and which will cause damage.

It took me fourteen years to realize that everyone gets damaged by something: too much confidence, not enough confidence, too much coddling, not enough love, fear of failure, fear of how others might view us when we succeed... Why were my early teens such a mess?

At fourteen years of age, I switched schools. Nothing is easy at fourteen, but I was lucky. My lifelong friend, Steve Goff, whose family lived directly behind my family's house, was going to the same school. Steve was already in with a fun group of guys, and they accepted me as I was because of Steve.

At a time when I was most emotionally vulnerable, this was the first group outside of my own family and Moose that had ever accepted me as I was. To this day, the wildest and most fun weekend of every year is our annual "Debacle at the Beach" with Pat O'Grady, Andy Monastra, Jack Mullen, Mark Forsythe, Joe Romano, Mike O'Donnell, Michael Doyle, Jim Costigan, and Steve Goff.

When I graduated college, I moved to Houston, TX for a couple of years. It was my first time living alone away from home. The day I arrived in Houston, I stayed at a Holiday Inn on Highway 59. It was there that I met a young, Cuban American couple from Miami named Jose and Mary Roque; their families had immigrated from Cuba. Jose and I met shooting hoops at a nearby basketball court.

A few weeks after I moved into an apartment complex, Ricky Byrd and Craig Townsend moved into the apartment next to mine. I guess we were all a little nervous, having left our homes in pursuit of some kind of unique adventure in a new city. They became family to me in Houston, and as we all recirculated later, they gave me families in Atlanta, Miami, and Houston.

Similarly, when I started POC Media, so many of the people I love are folks I met back in the 90s and early 2000s, people who supported my business and believed in me when I wasn't such a sure bet. There are too many to mention in one book, but the time I have spent and still spend with these people has shaped—and continues to shape—my life. Some I live with on the road, most I dine with when I'm in their cities, and without any one of them, my life would be far less complete.

One time, when one of my employees unexpectedly ran out of money while visiting clients in LA, Stephanie and Matt Cohen ran downtown on a minute's notice and gave my guy a thousand dollars... I think they knew I would pay them back, but that was one of the first (and fortunately one of the only) times anyone had done something like that for me.

Later, at a time when my business needed credibility, Julie Greenwald (Co-Chair of Atlantic Records), Jason Flom (Chairman of Lava Records), Greg Ham (President of Forefront), Scott Robinson (Founder of Dualtone), Mike Dungan (Chairman of UMG Nashville), Bruce Resnikoff (CEO of UMe), and Bruce Kirkland (Founder of Tsunami Entertainment) all did on-camera testimonials for POC Media's promotional video. These are all people who were willing to support me at a time when it felt like everything I had bet on could collapse within seconds. Their endorsements were critical to my being able to stay in the game.

Shortly after we put the new promotional video together, an executive from one of the major label groups expressed puzzlement as to why my company had been hired. Truth be told, I think I must have just reminded her of someone she didn't like. Next thing you know, I'm hearing rumors that this person is trying to get my company blown out of the label group.

When I asked VPs Don Terbush, Tom Rowland, and the late greats Pat Lawrence and Bob Mercer why this person didn't like me, all of my problems at the label gradually went away. I don't know if they confronted the person or just said nice things about me, but I likely would not have stayed in business without their intervention.

There was a time when I was facing both challenges and opportunities, desperately in need of both mentorship and some financial support to make sure I could stay in the game

When I was desperately trying to work my way into NASCAR, a woman named Jill McPhee (now Jill D'Alessandro) introduced me to a handful of people—many of whom still work at NASCAR in Charlotte, many of whom are running other companies, and all of whom, including Jill and her amazing husband Keith, are still close friends.

That one relationship led to the unexpected blessing of friends who, for years, have given me the opportunity to do what I love most for a living. My experiences with a number of executives within television networks and production teams created a similar ripple effect that continued—and continues—to open the door for POC Media across multiple sports broadcast outlets.

We all know someone who just manages to end up in the middle of everything, either through their relationships, their intelligence, a great personality, or just a unique ability to spot opportunities. Perhaps it's some combination of all of these. For me, one such person is Johnny Rose. Johnny worked for DreamWorks in Nashville, TN.

One day, we were about to head out to lunch, and he showed me a video of a new artist on DreamWorks Nashville. I liked the song and passed a few comments regarding how impressed I was with both the woman's talent and the production on the music. Later that evening, Johnny invited me to dinner with the artist and her record producer, Andrew Gold, one of my all-time favorite musicians. Earlier that day, while driving to the Philly airport, I had been listening to Linda Ronstadt's Hasten Down the Wind CD, which featured Andrew on several instruments.

Meeting Andrew, I immediately started babbling about how much I loved his music and his session piano work on "Someone to Lay Down Beside Me," as well as his dueling guitar work with Waddy Wachtel on "That'll Be The Day;" so much so that I actually forgot to tell the artist how much I enjoyed her music. Andrew started laughing and gave me a big hug, saying, "You'll never know how much I needed to hear that today!"

It was Johnny that introduced me to a young Jimmy Wayne back in 2004, just prior to the release of "Paper Angel." It was also Johnny Rose who, one evening, asked if I wanted to come over to Ocean Way Recording Studio after dinner with him and some friends. We all ended up singing on Toby Keith's "I Love This Bar". I've still got the platinum album plaque in my office. If I ever start a cruise line, I want Johnny to be the cruise director!

And if I ever need a navigator, I'll want my friends Andy & Leslie Price to help steer the ship. In addition to being brilliant, wonderful friends, loving parents to their children, amazing grandparents, and genuine forces for good in this world, Andy and Leslie were willing to bet on me at a time when very few others would consider jumping in.

When I needed financial support because the banks weren't ready to extend my terms, Andy and Leslie were willing to take the risk. And when I needed grace, because perhaps the banks were correct, Andy and Leslie extended and eventually forgave debt, which in and of itself is an extraordinary act. But beyond that, they never brought it up again, but rather continued to encourage me to stay in the game and to forgive myself as they had forgiven me . . . sounds a little like a prayer I'm familiar with. Needless to say, Andy and Leslie continue to be trusted, loving advisors and friends . . . really more like family.

There is nothing I would not do for my friends and family; they mean the world to me, and here's the amazing revelation: in hindsight, my greatest moments of emotional flux, the most unsettling of times, produced the most meaningful relationships in my life, including the one with my wife. And here's the lovely side-effect of friendships: they are like trees with roots that run deep and branches that run wide. They lead to more friendships, which are what life is all about.

We've all heard the expression "Choose your friends wisely." My corollary to that rule is to "Be a good friend." It's hard to actually choose wisely; we all change. But being a good friend can change someone's life, and we never actually know how close that person is to falling off the edge. I'm so grateful to my friends for the times they knowingly or unwittingly brought me back from the edge.

The Get / The Recap

Emotional flux doesn't feel good, but it can bring the most beautiful relationships, emotions, and love into life. We never feel more alive than when we're right on the edge.

Flux happens when we're giving it our best with everything on the line. Embrace flux!

Go easy on kids. They know not what they do. Sometimes a wise word from the right person can change everything in a very positive way.

GETTING IT

We'll never know what kind of impact we have on some people until we meet them on the other side. Play it safe and be kind.

Chapter 6
Reframing Opportunity

Years ago, I got into the habit of asking my wife to check business emails that I thought might be too direct before I hit "send." Dot would always agree to read them, but she always added "If you have to ask, you already know." That's an interesting take on life in general. When we reframe the picture and consider seeing every challenge as an opportunity, we're more empowered to succeed. Somehow every question, every challenge, carries with it the answer along with a new form of enlightenment.

About fifteen years ago, I lined up a series of branded concerts at NCAA football games and some non-traditional venues, thinking I could use the sponsored events to generate exposure for some recording artists that I was helping. Once everything was set up, it became clear that my artist plan wasn't going to work. I needed a more established, brand-friendly artist who could entertain a diverse group of football fans while charming the sponsors and their retailers. The sponsor was one of the world's largest producers and distributors of soft drinks, so this was an important project, and I wasn't budgeted for the kind of artist they wanted.

Years earlier, I had met a young woman of whom I had been a fan for years; her name is Jennifer Paige. Years prior to our casual breakfast meeting, she had recorded the smash hit, "Crush," which made it to #1 in sixteen countries. Having met a lot of artists, I tend to be numb to stats and chart positions; they're just arbitrary forms of measurement that support bragging rights. I'm generally more interested in who an artist IS rather than how well the artist's songs did on the charts.

Meeting Jennifer was like a breath of fresh air. Jennifer is one of the kindest, most thoughtful, most talented, and most intelligent artists I've ever met. That morning, as we left our breakfast at the Puffy Muffin in Nashville, I remember thinking, "I hope we get to do something together someday; I'll bet she would be fun to work with."

Flashing forward several years to my NCAA dilemma, scrambling for an artist to perform on our branded tour, I reached out to Jennifer thinking she might direct me to someone she thought would be a good fit. To my delight, Jennifer offered to do the tour herself, provided I could come up with a competent backing band on my shoestring budget.

My client was delighted; Jennifer delivered like a champ every night, and she even allowed my son to play lead guitar in the band, giving my son his first experience in a touring band. My son has gone on to record and produce multiple albums for himself and others, landing more than a dozen music licensing syncs in television programming, commercials, video games, and DVDs.

Jennifer and I continue to be close, as we have worked on several projects together over the years. She now has a wonderful husband and an adorable daughter, and Jennifer continues to be one of my most trusted mentors and the most grounded artist I know. I'm grateful to call her my friend.

Sometimes, reframing means changing our predisposed positions on a subject. Back in the late 1990s, Contemporary Christian music was a tight industry housed primarily in Brentwood, TN, a nearby suburb of Nashville. When POC Media was spearheading sports-promotions for Virgin Records' artists (bands like Spice Girls, Blur, and Crystal Method), I was encouraged to touch base with the EMI Christian Music Group's hippest CCM label, Forefront Records. Personally, I liked a lot of Contemporary Christian music, but I was at a loss to see how it might fit into sports arenas that specifically worked to avoid religion and politics.

Among Forefront's artists was a rap-rock trio called DC Talk. Their big single was a song called "Jesus Freak." I loved the band, but I saw no way of convincing sports leagues to jump on the song. Luckily, when I'm in doubt, I just assume the artist knows their craft better than I do, so I threw deep, and we were able to get the song played in a handful of key NHL arenas. At the time, I was getting a little push back from some arenas, but I wanted to keep the folks at Virgin happy, so I kept pushing.

The result of that leap of faith continues to define the POC Media story and has become a cornerstone in my life. It launched friendships with Forefront GM Allan Hardin and his wife Shauna—their home is my home away from home whenever I'm in Nashville; I literally live with them when I'm in The Music City—as well as with Forefront's

President Greg Ham. Both Allan and Greg have been my precious friends and mentors for more than two decades.

When DC Talk's charismatic leader TobyMac went solo, he and his label continued to allow us to work his music for sports syncs. Toby even let me produce one of his concerts at the 2008 NASCAR Bank of America 500, giving POC Media a level of street cred in both the NASCAR and Contemporary Christian worlds that would have been improbable to secure on our own.

Reframing a situation sometimes just means refusing to accept the answer "no." Two occasions come to mind when I was licensing music for national commercial campaigns on fixed budgets. Out of respect for the parties involved, I'm leaving out the names of the brands and artists.

The first was for a song from a classic rock icon of whom I am a big fan. Apparently, the licensing budget I was proposing was sufficiently below what that artist generally licensed music for. His publishers, label, and attorney did not want to present my proposal to him. So, I asked his attorney for backstage passes to one of his concerts so I could travel to his gig at a nearby city and make the proposal myself, keeping everyone else from incurring the wrath of the artist if he ended up being offended. Plus, I brought my secret weapons to the show: my wife and kids.

Prior to the show, we went backstage, and the artist was absolutely wonderful with my family, charming my wife (in fact, flirting with her!), and inspiring both my kids to pursue careers in music, something they've both done to a great degree of success. He then had his assistant bring my family to their seats while he and I had a short conversation in his dressing room. He politely pointed out that my proposed number was a bit low, and he asked why I thought it was fair.

After striking out on why he should accept my offer and realizing that this deal was not going to happen, I told him something very personal that was 100% true and sincere. I said, "you know that woman I'm married to—the one you were flirting with in such an adorable way—our second date was seeing you and your band in Cherry Hill, New Jersey [at a specific venue and on a specific date that I named];" I even told him what the sign in front of the drum kit said. He smiled and said, "you were one of those early ones... so you really are a life-long fan... let's do it!" Perhaps I should bring my wife to more meetings!

On another occasion, there was a song that I thought would be perfect for a commercial being produced for a brand I was representing. I made an offer, again probably less than the market value, but I was working with a tight budget. The person with the authority to license the song told me that I was too low.

He and I are good friends, so I knew he was being honest, but I only had the amount that I had, and I never negotiate. To me, negotiating is just two parties lying to each other until they reach a number that neither of them wanted in the first place. So, I never negotiate; I only offer what I believe is fair and mutually beneficial.

I told my friend that once I left, I would call a different rightsholder for another specific song, and I would offer them the same amount. He told me that he believed my offer would be rejected by his competitor as well. I knew he was probably correct, as both songs were iconic, but I also knew that his competitor's front-line labels didn't have as many current hit singles as my friend's label group did.

So, I started making the one-hour drive to his competitor's office, and called the other rightsholder from the car, fully prepared for a "no." When he delivered on the anticipated response, I asked him to consider how many employees his department might lay off at year-end, and how that risk might be mitigated by agreeing on this deal. I asked him to write down their names, and to thoughtfully consider how those conversations would feel: "Merry Christmas, you're fired!" Dilemmas and solutions become much more discernable when the consequences feel personal.

That gentleman laughed, came up with a couple of creative, non-consequential "carve-outs" for the deal, and within minutes of my arriving at his office, we collaborated to make it happen. I am still good friends with both of these gentlemen, and I believe this specific deal improved my working relationships with both of them as well as with the brand and the managers of the recording artist whose music we licensed.

I never cease to be amazed at the inherent goodness in people—all people. I'll bet that sounds silly to some folks, but I can't begin to tell you the number of times I've seen people act against their own agendas because they would rather do what's right.

Doing what's right or combining one's passion

with a worthy cause can bring about the most interesting reframing of opportunities, and sometimes, this reframing can lead to lasting friendships, a sense of community within a common cause, and great memories that last a lifetime.

There is a college in Warrensburg, Missouri: The University of Central Missouri (UCM), for which I have a soft spot in my heart. I never went there as a student, but I've produced a handful of concerts in their field house, and I have genuinely come to love several members of the faculty as well as the catering, physical, and athletic departments.

One woman in particular is both a dear friend and a courageous inspiration to me. To call Beth Rutt a cancer survivor would be a failure to adequately express who Beth is; Beth is a CANCER CRUSHER! I've watched Beth run the student activities department at UCM while battling cancer, dealing with sepsis, and successfully managing what most people would consider crises. To Beth, it's all just life, and Beth makes everyone's life better. She is literally a beacon of hope and inspiration, and she's funny as all get-out!

Shortly after the riots in Ferguson, Missouri, followed by some issues at another state university in Missouri, Beth asked me if we could put together a concert specifically designed to promote multicultural unity at UCM. We concluded that the best way to do this would be to book two bands that were dramatically different: one band intended to appeal to hip hop fans, and one band to appeal to punk rock fans. We would then use the artist cross-promotion and interaction between these two culturally diverse bands to promote unity on campus.

The two acts that we picked were hip hop stars Rae Sremmurd and Warped Tour main-stagers, The Summer Set. The two bands and their associated audiences could not have been much more diverse. Luckily for me, and thanks to my good friend, mentor, and Super-Agent, Zach Iser, I had already produced a show with Rae Sremmurd, so we had some nice history together, and I had met The Summer Set on the Warped Tour. Both bands consist of good people, which is always a good starting point.

I had to make several over-the-top requests of both bands; unreasonably cutting down their hospitality riders, asking them to post things about the other band to create the sense of unity we were pushing for the event, asking them to hang for student meet and greets for those who helped us set up the venue, and even asking them to modify their tech riders.

Similarly, I had to make a lot of requests from the local police to be particularly patient with an audience I was concerned might become unruly... I did not want our concert showing up on the national news and embarrassing the university.

Every party embraced the challenge and accommodated all of my requests, making things run smoothly and profitably, and creating one of the best concerts I've ever seen.

Producing concerts is actually a very easy job. If you can follow a checklist and make sure the artists show up when they say they will, then you can produce a concert. The challenge is that when something goes wrong, it frequently goes very wrong, and people lose money—sometimes a lot of money—and then they become very unhappy. Unhappiness has consequences. This is why there is only a handful of people producing large concerts in the United States. Once you are a proven entity, you become part of a small club: the men and women who can be trusted to book, promote, present, and produce concerts.

My approach to producing events and concerts

is to surround myself with trustworthy people who work without limits, get along with everyone, and are good at heading off problems before they arise, people like Andrew Roomberg, Christian Orellana, Rob Evanoff, Devon O'Connor, and Christian O'Connor. Then my job is to figure out what that one thing is that might go wrong to ruin everything.

The obvious hot spots are rigging motors or trusses falling down, bad sound, a poor stage surface, insufficient power, or community code violations... these are parameters that are easily controlled by a solid team.

To me, the most dangerous thing that cannot be controlled is media interpretation of what is happening. Bad press can make a good event look bad. Weak security can give the press bad things to talk about. Too tight of security or too many rules can upset an audience and create exactly the effect one is trying to avoid. So, my job is to find that one thing and make sure it does not happen.

In Warrensburg, that one thing was that I wanted to make sure there were no confrontations among audience members or between the fans and law enforcement that could cause news agencies or students to turn against the police. Keep in mind that I was asking the police to provide safety for a college audience that might be high, drunk, or both. We were also creating a very high-energy event where the artists would be encouraging the crowd to get wild, within a couple hundred miles of where there had recently been a great deal of civil unrest.

The result was one of the most beautiful evenings I've ever seen, largely due to an incredible student body, a passionate and committed student activities department and faculty, two great bands, and an understanding and flexible police department. Thousands of college students of various ethnicities were partying together, the police were helping to prevent audience members from being pushed against the 45-degree stage barricades, security teams were tossing free bottles of water to the fans, and Rae Sremmurd and The Summer Set were rocking Warrensburg like it had never been rocked before.

At the end of the evening, we had zero arrests, zero injuries, zero insurance claims, glowing news coverage, and thousands of students taking to the campus and to the internet with joy and enthusiasm. It was a WIN!

My experience is that every question carries its

own answer, every challenge brings with it an even greater opportunity, and when we reframe challenges as opportunities, life works better.

The Get / The Recap

If we have to ask, we probably already know the answer... a little soul-searching can be useful.

Most of our best opportunities show up dressed as problems. I've often said that every deal I've ever closed started with the word "no."

We don't always get what we ask for, but we never get what we don't ask for. Ask for what you want... sometimes you have to call someone you had breakfast with, sometimes you have to ask an artist to let you produce his concert, sometimes you have to get yourself backstage to ask for a licensing deal, and sometimes you have to tell your friends to make business personal.

Negotiating is the process of two people being dishonest with each other to arrive at a mutually unacceptable number. Never negotiate; just be honest with a win-win proposal and be ready to walk away.

Find someone like Beth Rutt who can inspire, motivate, and guide you toward excellence.

Chapter 7
Tuning In on the Insanity of Love

Owning a business with clients in the sports and music industries, I've had the good fortune of meeting a large number of the people I admire most throughout the world. The one person whom I've admired most as a living saint in my lifetime was Mother Teresa of Calcutta; and unfortunately, I never met Mother Teresa, but I know someone who did. I have heard stories about her from my friend and read books about her as well, and I have found her approach to life quite motivating. More than just exhibiting kindness, Mother Teresa made the point that every successful person I've ever studied has demonstrated: "If you can't do everything, then just do something."

"If you can't do everything, then just do something." When I first heard this, I thought it was a little simple—and obvious. But then I started thinking about my own life and asking myself the question: "what should I be doing?" As a man living in western society, like most other men, I had accepted values that dictated a career focus.

Interestingly enough, the people who have had the greatest impact on my life often don't seem to have a career focus. My mother-in-law has a fifth-grade formal education. I say this with pride, as she is one of the smartest people I've ever met. She spent a great deal of time helping a senior citizen by buying her groceries, helping to clean her apartment, and spending time with her so she wouldn't be alone.

My own mother dedicated most of her time to helping people, whether volunteering in hospitals as a candy-striper or helping relatives and non-relatives alike when they were ill, and often providing particularly heartfelt comfort while they were dying. Despite their work with others, both my mom and my mother-in-law always found time to help Dot and me, whether strategically and tangibly by lending an ear, or in their help with our children. It was a "win-win-win" by which we all benefitted.

Likewise, my dad was always there for advice and help, probably more after his retirement than before, and I ended up having a much stronger bond with my father as an adult than I ever remember having while growing up.

PAT O'CONNOR

It was on a summer afternoon in Nashville, while having lunch with a good friend, a Vice President of Marketing for a major record label, that I was floored to hear that in her spare time, my friend had helped start the Byzantine Catholic Church in Nashville. Feeling somewhat inadequate for my own lack of impact, I suggested that my greatest accomplishment was getting some country music videos played in hockey arenas—not exactly the kind of thing that gets one a "well done, good and faithful servant" shout-out.

But my friend, either out of kindness or some sense of awareness, told me that I had probably had some one-on-one impact with several of my acquaintances as well as my family, and if I kept my eyes open, I would be in tune with opportunities as they came along. I realized she was probably right, but I also recognized that as a middle-aged man, it was time for me to stop accidentally having an impact, and to start planning my life with one goal in mind: hearing "well done, good and faithful servant" at the end of the game.

This is where that wave stuff comes back into play. In reading books on Eastern philosophy and trying to integrate some of the practical ideas into my own approach, I found a lot more correlations than I expected to discover. I also found some striking parallels to my quantum physics studies.

What I've been calling The Great Unknown, my Eastern friends call The Source, Universal Intelligence, Higher Self, The Over Soul, The Universe, or The Infinite Field of Correlations. Like my Eastern friends, I have found that through deep prayer and meditation, I can establish contact with God. When I say contact, I mean a relationship in which not only can I reach out to God, but God also reaches back in a way that creates the feeling of a divine presence or what some might call a peaceful, personal connection in my life. I'm talking about a sense of certainty that I'm connected with something far greater than myself, and a belief that if I sincerely ask for guidance, then the scenarios leading my desires will actually drive me to have a positive impact on the world and on others. While some of my Eastern friends don't see the God-Pat relationship as anything personal, I found their approach surprisingly similar to my own.

For me, the process of establishing contact is six-fold. First, I clarify what matters most. Second, I get a clear picture of what things would look like if I could bring about what I want most.

Third, I marinate on that picture with a desire that borders on obsession. Fourth, I pray for guidance in desiring what will most please God, and I ask for the faith and wisdom to accept and implement that guidance, ready to accept God's will regardless of whether it matches my request.

Having formed that picture of my intention, and having asked for God's help and guidance, my fifth step is to meditate and take my mind to the level of Pure Energy, where there are no words, no labels, no attachment, no ego. I quietly revel in the knowledge that God has everything under control, and I am now awaiting God's guidance and God's blessings. In short, without presuming I've got God's will all figured out, I thank God for the love, mercy, and power in my life.

It is in this state that I reach the sixth phase: surrender. I release my emotional attachment to my will and live in absolute faith that God has things under control and my life will be better for it... you know, like, "Thy will be done." Hey, I never said it was original!

A cynic might point out that it is impossible for this formula to fail, since I'm claiming to be happy no matter what happens, but the reality is that something magical happens. At a level of synchronicity that defies statistical probability, events have often begun to move in the direction of my prayers.

Short meditations have resulted in people with whom I need to get in touch calling me from their cell phones within minutes of my prayers. I've had chance meetings in restaurants after praying to casually connect with certain business contacts. I have attracted into my life circumstances over which I had no apparent control, and yet events played out as I had visualized them. At the extreme limits of this process, I've experienced inexplicable healings and seen what I believe to be the same in others.

The first key to realizing the reality at which I've aimed has been the establishment of a target. The target comes from locking in on the plan in time to do something with it, and the ability to see the target clearly comes from LOVE.

Ah, you didn't see that coming? For years, I didn't see it coming either. I met my wife when I was fifteen years old, and it took eight years and three rejected proposals to get her to marry me. How crazy is that? At twenty-three years of age, Dot and I made a life-long commitment, assuming we had any idea of what life would be all about as we got older. We assumed that we somehow understood who each of us would be by the time we were in our sixties, and somehow, we were right! That is the insanity of LOVE!

When two people suspend all disbelief and just go for it, we laugh and think they're so adorable. But isn't that how miracles happen? We wrap ourselves in so many rules and we assume that certain things have to go right. We assume that we need to work our way through a process and that if we don't achieve certain goals by a certain age, somehow we are losing the game.

There's a great scene in the movie Moneyball where a player who never makes it to second base decides to try, and he falls rounding first. The first baseman looks like he's laughing at the embarrassed guy for falling, but he's actually laughing because the overweight player struggling to regain his balance on what he thinks is a single, has actually hit the ball sixty feet over the centerfield fence for a home run.

I love that metaphor for life! Sometimes we get so wrapped up in the steps of the moment, so mired in our inability to round first base, that we miss the opportunity to watch the ball leave the park. Honestly, how many home runs have you failed to celebrate because you were worried about rounding first base?

It's so easy to skip the suspension of all disbelief and the anticipation of something better. One of my mentors once told me at a time when things were not looking good for my business, that my recent failures were "terrific." Puzzled by the cavalier attitude he was taking toward my obvious failures, I pointed out that I was on the brink of a disaster. Again, he said, "Pat, that's terrific!"

Fed up with his mocking, I asked what was so "terrific" about my problems. He pointed out that the story of some kid growing up with no problems, making money, finding a nice life-partner, being healthy, and never having challenges, was not the stuff that great books and movies are made of.

He reminded me that the best sporting events are when the score keeps changing and the fans are on the edges of their seats. He said, "You have so many fans in Heaven, Pat, give 'em a show worth watching! Then use your trials and the way you overcome them to make someone else's journey easier. In the meantime, please shut up and go help somebody! It will take your mind off of YOU."

The suspension of disbelief; it's the spice of life, it's the insanity of LOVE!

The Get / The Recap

I like to ask myself, "What am I doing? And is what I'm doing moving me closer to or farther from what I would like to accomplish?"

I try to always do something. We can't do everything, but we can do something that moves us toward what we want most.

If a person can't figure out what matters most, they can mentally move to the end of their life and work backwards until they arrive at the present situation. When one stands at the end of life looking back, it feels like looking backward at a simple maze from overhead. The correct and only appropriate path should be clear. The right priorities should be obvious. If one can project to that "end-of-life" point and identify the right priorities on the way back to "now," one's path to the finish line should be much more direct.

Be kind to those who think they have God all figured out, but be open to the reality that wisdom arrives from many places. Wisdom is often delivered by those who see and live life from a very different place than you.

We are somehow connected with God, and one's faith in that connection is often more important than one's thorough understanding of God.

LOVE matters. LOVE steps into the gap between desire and action, cutting through the cord between hope and destiny and providing a bridge to—and a line of communication with—our Creator.

The suspending of all disbelief in a dream is the insanity of LOVE, and the bond that brings forgiveness, patience, and compassion to the innately selfish heart. Never give up on LOVE.

Chapter 8
Love and the Other Cheek

My belief in people from an early age may have left me a little naïve when I started POC Media. I grew up in the suburbs of Philadelphia, cutting lawns, working as a lab tech, and playing the piano in bars and studios. I was surrounded by a variety of people, ranging from bar owners to PhDs, to coaches, to studio engineers, to musicians, to landscapers, to instrument salesmen, to priests, to ministers, to the unhoused.

I grew up believing that people were basically good. I still believe that, but my work in the entertainment industry has also caused me to recognize that some people are just not good people. I'm not suggesting we should judge people's motives or morality; but I also don't believe in accepting bad behavior from another person just because they think they are entitled to be inconsiderate, or because they work in an industry with less rules than typical corporate America.

The opposing corollary to "good" vs. "not

good" is that it is too easy to misjudge people and to act with an incorrect predisposed bias. I've been guilty of it myself... sometimes devils look like angels, and sometimes the angels come in disguise to teach us. What follows are two of the first and one of the latter.

Early in my work with the NHL arenas, a seemingly well-respected representative of a small music publishing company threatened to sue me over something that was not an infringement of any kind. When I spoke directly with this person, he informed me that he had a lawyer on staff and that while he sort-of agreed that there was no legal infringement or damage done, it would cost me more to fight him in court than it would to just settle by paying him some money.

In some circles, this is called creative revenue management. I believe decent people refer to it as extortion. But I also knew that he was correct about the financial implications. What he had overlooked was that I was working for record labels, the very companies on which his company depended to record his songs.

When I explained my dilemma to one label executive, I was told not to worry about it; my label friend would weigh in... and did he ever! I received a call from the extortionist about ten minutes later, requesting that I intervene on his behalf so that he didn't lose the label as a client.

Interestingly enough, I was not angry with the guy; I was more in a state of disbelief that someone who had threatened to extort money from me moments ago would now be asking for my help. So, I just hung up on him and went back to whatever I was working on. When he called back a few minutes later, he seemed genuinely shaken by the prospect that I was going to leave him hung out to dry.

So, I told him that I would put in a good word for him, provided he would call all of his friends and tell them what had just happened. My reasoning was that I believe good people stick together and bad people tend to hang out together. Needless to say, I can't always identify them; so, this fellow could be my PR guy to the rest of the would-be thugs. I refer to them as "would-be thugs" because they aren't really thugs; they're jerks. And jerks who act like thugs generally get hurt.

I never had that kind of problem again with a rightsholder, so I guess this guy was good at PR. I've bumped into him a few times since, and there's never been an issue or even a mention of the incident. In the words of Michael Corleone of The Godfather fame, it was just business to him. However, to me, it was personal, and it was an eye-opener as to how some people manage to compartmentalize morality, and how some of these people manage to maintain the respect of others in their industry.

Notwithstanding everything I said about Christianity in an earlier chapter, I do believe that sometimes turning the other cheek is not the best first move. I believe in forgiving, I don't believe in forgetting, and when someone tries to hurt you, I think it's okay to leave the perpetrator with a lesson that encourages them not to forget.

I remember hearing a professional hockey player pass the comment that you don't need to immediately retaliate when someone takes a cheap shot. But at some point in the game, that guy will be skating with his head down, and a clean check will deliver the message effectively to that player, to the rest of his team, and to your own team.

Three lessons that I've learned from dealing with jerks and thugs are that appeasement never works, word travels quickly when you hit back, and the harder you hit, the less likely you'll have to deal with those jerks or thugs again in the future.

Once POC Media became proficient in producing concerts, some of our corporate clients began asking us to plan, stage, produce, and manage their corporate conferences and events, ranging from branded concerts to franchisee conventions and executive presentations. These events generally take place in large hotels or conference centers, and certain cities have reputations for being either more or less producer-friendly for conventions.

While producing concerts, I learned something interesting about promoters: these men and women were true pioneers and entrepreneurs back in the day, and pioneers and entrepreneurs are impossible to intimidate. I've had the good fortune of working with a handful of these pioneers, and while they have all been wonderful with me, I have heard enough stories and seen enough scuffles to know that many of these people are much tougher than I could ever hope to be.

Fortunately, my experience working on live concert events has always been smooth, largely because our events tend to be branded, sponsored, soft-ticket shows. In other words, these are concerts that take place after a sporting event, at a festival, or in association with a retailer. Our other shows tend to be at colleges, which generally involve committed teachers combined with a young and pleasant student activities team.

In all of these cases, my work never competes with any local or national promoters. In fact, we frequently hire the locals as consultants to help navigate code enforcement and on-the-ground issues that may come up.

Once we started producing corporate conferences, I found that there are people who sometimes offer to provide "security" for an event. Ironically, concert security has always been easy to deal with, but for some reason, when it comes to convention centers and hotels, I would find these peculiar folks forcefully suggesting that we needed their "help" at simple corporate events.

Of course, they don't really mean that they will help with the event; they are actually threatening to intimidate the crew or to destroy the equipment if they are not paid an extortion fee.

The first time this happened, I was in a city where we enjoyed solid working relationships with all of the relevant parties within the venue, code-enforcement, and security worlds. A large, well-dressed man wearing a black suit with a black shirt and a black tie approached me. He informed me that I would need his associates to ensure the security of our equipment in the hotel ballroom.

When I asked if he worked with the hotel, he said, "No." Assuming he might be from a union, I mentioned that we actually had a couple of union members working the event, even though the hotel itself was a non-union facility. My experience has been that union workers know what they're doing, are well-trained, and work well with both venues and crews.

This guy didn't seem like a well-trained fellow who would get along well with others. He told me that he was not affiliated with either the hotels or locals. In other words, this was a shake-down.

I took out my iPhone and pulled up the name and cell phone number of a person from that town who would be immediately recognized as someone with experience, someone to be taken seriously, someone whose name I assumed this guy might know. I said that I would call this person. If this person told me to pay the guy, I would do it. If this person didn't know this guy, then we would need to have a less comfortable conversation.

The guy in the suit became visibly less comfortable, asking me not to make the call. Perhaps I should have just sent the guy away, but feeling somewhat offended by his attempt to intimidate me, I "hired" him to handle security. This is to say that I handed him two hundred dollars, asked him to sit in the corner of the ballroom, and instructed him to keep an eye on things and to look out for possible troublemakers until we spoke again. I pointed out that since he was holding the two hundred I had just paid him, we were now in business together and I expected him to "look out" for my team.

Things get busy when you're setting up stages, projectors, lights, sound systems, and chairs, plus managing catering; it's easy to forget that someone is sitting in the corner. After about four hours, one of my subcontractors asked who the guy in the corner was. At this point, I realized that I had left a grown man sitting in the corner of a ballroom for four hours; he hadn't even used the restroom. I think he had it coming, but I was still a little embarrassed. as this flew in the face of everything I believe in terms of respecting people.

I walked over to him and told him that I really

only meant to make a point when I sent him to the corner, and that I had forgotten once I got busy. He seemed relieved and apologized for trying to steal from us. He tried to give me back the two hundred dollars, but at that point, I figured I kind of owed it to him. I also shared with him my belief that thugs and idiots like to flock together; I asked him to keep the money and to inform any other would-be shakedown artists that he knew they should avoid our hotel for the week.

Fortunately, in my three decades of running my own business, situations like those mentioned above tend to be few and far between. One of my favorite challenges in dealing with people actually ended up being a most rewarding weekend that restored my own faith in youth-at-risk and, in fact, probably helped some young men believe in themselves.

POC Media was producing a large concert with a major act at a NASCAR track. The concert would take place just prior to the race and would be staged between turns #1 and #2 at one of North America's superspeedways. In the last chapter, I mentioned that producing concerts is easy. There is one caveat to that truth: producing concerts in conjunction with sporting events is actually very challenging. There are several reasons for the challenges.

First, the fans are there to see a sporting event, meaning that the concert is a side show. Most artists, regardless of their stature in the entertainment industry, believe themselves to be much more than a side show. Their tour managers take their tech riders very seriously, and it is almost impossible to satisfy either a tech rider or a hospitality rider at an outdoor sports venue on a limited budget.

Second, there are staging restrictions at sports venues. One must be very careful with the field, the track, the court, the ice; the surfaces on which the sports take place. When a team owner pays an athlete millions of dollars, they expect that athlete to compete on a safe surface, free of indentations, cracks, holes, or any of the other joint-and-ligament-threatening surface disturbances that can be caused by a shoddy production team.

Third, there is an issue of where the stage can be placed to optimize power, sightlines, shelter, and artist access. And fourth, when you have forty-three stock cars driving at speeds approaching two hundred miles per hour, these drivers depend heavily on their spotters. Every time you watch a

NASCAR race, there is some kind of skid or accident that can produce a life-or-death situation.

When there is an accident on the track, there are a few seconds between the wreck and the caution lights coming on. During that few seconds, the drivers are flying through smoke and debris, unable to see the cars ahead of them. They depend on the spotters to tell them to break left or right, or to gun it straight ahead to get past the danger. All of this is to say that sightlines at a NASCAR race are critical. And since the races are televised, there is a real deadline, a specific time by which the sightlines need to be cleared.

Operating on a tight budget and setting up a Stageline outdoor stage with sound and lights, I needed to make sure we had enough strong people to get the stage up and down in time for the concert and the race. I brought my own crew, and I took a chance on a group of young men, some of whom one might label as at-risk youth, to help us raise and lower the stage along with the sound and lights.

We were told by "experts" that it would take several hours to set everything up and then ninety minutes to get the stage down low enough to open the necessary sightlines prior to the race. Unfortunately, cold, windy weather the night before the race made the set-up challenging, and we would only have forty-five minutes to get the stage down prior to the race to allow the spotters to do their job.

We were paying the young men a reasonable amount of money and giving them tickets to the race. I guess I felt like I was doing somewhat of a good deed, and I was comfortable that with the number of guys we had, the staging would be no problem. As a handful of the young men began to make light of their responsibilities, their apathy became contagious, and before I knew it, I had a group of guys who seemed to be doing their best to convince us that those who had labeled the young men as at-risk may have been on target.

Generally, I have trouble firing anyone, but we were under the gun, and I knew that there were a couple of ringleaders in the group that were holding the team back.

Around midnight on the evening before the concert, we were already way behind schedule. I lined up the crew in the middle of the infield, reviewed our mission, and asked everyone to do one of two things: either commit to meeting the challenge or get out of our way and go home.

I also offered to pay everyone their full rate regardless of which option they decided to take. One of the lead smart-asses flipped me the bird and said he would like to take his money and go home. I thanked him for his candor, told him that his attitude would not be missed, and asked the rest of the team if they wished to join their fearless leader in what I could only imagine would be a life of under-achievement, loneliness, and regret. I added that if they'd prefer to prove the nay-sayers wrong, they could stick around and help. Everyone else decided to stay.

As I was walking the disgruntled guy to where his ride could come and get him, he crudely expressed his disappointment with my style. I told him that he might be right. Perhaps my fuse was too short, perhaps life was unfair, perhaps we all need to learn to deal with unreasonable people, and perhaps I was one of those unreasonable people. But in this moment, tonight was all that he had, and he just walked away from it in order to preserve his own ego.

I asked him how many times he'd ever followed through on something, and how many times he had ever considered the possibility that he might be responsible for his own failures. I asked if he would explain tonight's failure as someone else's fault and continue a pattern that was unlikely to lead to a lifetime of achievement, relationships, happiness, and a sense of self-worth. I asked if he had any idea what it might feel like to go the distance, win or lose, to stay in the fight until it's finished, and to know that he had given it his best.

I also suggested that if he was open to changing his mind, I would be open to changing mine. This guy ended up staying the night, working hard, and actually being a positive leader among the young guys.

We did get the stage up in time, and we brought it down in thirty-five minutes, leaving ten minutes to spare before the track went live on television. The crew got to meet the band and hang out for the NASCAR race; a few even met some drivers. I realized that what I've always preached was true: everyone has the capacity for greatness.

I learned to stop under-budgeting concert productions and to be more careful about who we bring in as subcontractors. I also learned that at least one and probably more of those guys realized they could deliver under pressure and accomplish what they set out to do... the past was history. On that night, every one of those guys was a winner, and they all knew it!

Here's what hit me after that concert: that publisher, that guy in the suit trying to shake me down, that kid who went from zero to hero at the NASCAR track, and every kid that society gives up on, they all have the capacity for greatness from the moment they come to understand it. Good parents know this instinctively, and they never give up on their kids. They pray, they work, and they do whatever it takes to help their children navigate this world.

Some people turn the other cheek out of love. Some people tell themselves they're turning the other cheek out of love, when in fact, they are just insecure and afraid of hurting someone's feelings. Maybe they want to be their kids' best friend rather than a parent. Some people turn the other cheek because they are afraid of what might happen to them if they confront evil head on. It's so much easier to speak of love than it is to confront fear. It's easier to say that we're above fighting than it is to risk losing the fight.

So, I've stopped turning the other cheek. Not because I believe in retaliation, but because I've come to understand that appeasement does not work. It's one of the foundations for my own faith. I believe that God is real, and I believe that love is our highest value. Unfortunately, evil is also real—call it fear, call it doubt, call it a lack of love—and sometimes evil must be confronted with something stronger than the other cheek.

Love is what brings us all the capacity to meet our challenges, while evil is the voice of fear within that prevents us from having the courage to follow through. Always choose love, and always crush fear.

The Get / The Recap

Turning the other cheek is not always a good idea.

Evil people have a remarkable gift for compartmentalizing morality in a way that deceives both themselves and others.

Appeasement never works.

Word travels quickly when you hit back. It's always best to avoid fights, but if you are going to hit, hit hard.

Respect the pioneers, entrepreneurs, and your elders; they're probably tougher than they look.

Never underestimate the ability of a damaged

young person to learn, adjust, overcome adversity, and deliver when it matters most.

Love = Good | Fear = Evil... We can defeat fear with love. Bank on it!

Chapter 9
Meeting the Challenge

    I have been blessed with an interesting variety of mentors. They include: a deceased ninety-year-old entrepreneur for whom I used to work; an entrepreneur, fitness guru, author, motivational powerhouse, and former NBA team president; a seasoned mergers-and-acquisitions mogul, former bar owner, and successful agent for professional athletes; a deceased, seasoned artist manager who handled one of the 70s and 80s supergroups; a recording engineer and studio owner who created a sound that drove a 70s R&B craze; two lawyers—married to each other—with a wide range of experience in business and people management; a venture capitalist, who became an entertainment-licensing entrepreneur; a humble Italian immigrant whose wisdom and street sense would put most MBAs to shame; a concert promoter and founder of one of the longest-lasting traveling concert festival tours that sold more than five hundred thousand tickets every summer for twenty-five years; my dad, whose experience and love for business, life, and family, produced concise, and sometimes biting input—but it was always accurate, timely, and well-intentioned; an equity-fund giant, rumored to be worth hundreds of millions of dollars; and a minister, who stepped into my life as an adolescent, and has been there as both a friend and mentor for both my family and myself ever since.

I have frequently been told that I'm lucky to have these mentors. It is true that I'm lucky, both for their friendship and for their wisdom. But the fact that I became close with these mentors is no accident. I have always believed that the way to produce successful results is to understand what makes successful people successful, and then apply it to my own life. One of my mentors expresses it well by saying, "Everyone knows what successful people know. Winners do what successful people do."

So how do we identify a successful person, and what do successful people do? I define success as a sense of balance and passion in constantly moving toward a noble goal. I believe most successful people exhibit the same characteristics I see in all of my mentors.

Successful people know what they want.

Successful people don't believe they will succeed; they know they will succeed.

It is almost impossible to get a successful person to focus on anything other than what they want. They know that we tend to move in the direction of our thoughts, and if we focus on what we fear or dislike, we will continue to attract more of the same into our lives.

Successful people enjoy raising the bar.

And successful people, to quote Winston Churchill, "never, never, never, never give up." In other words, successful people know how to hold on to a vision.

Early in the growth of my business, when most reasonable people would not have considered investing in POC Media, I was frequently asked when my company would turn a profit and how I was dealing with these hard times. Ironically, I thought I was doing rather well.

Despite the fact that my family of four lived in a modest house with two very old cars and my business was generating negative cash flow, my mentors encouraged me. They reminded me to hold the vision for my business and family. They told me that if I stayed focused on the end game, the details would take care of themselves.

The mission for my business was to develop the world's most creative integrated marketing company with a presence in the sports, music, entertainment, and corporate worlds, and I intended to do this in a way that created a fun environment for employees and clients alike. I committed to only enter into working relationships where my clients could see a measurable return on their marketing investment, and I insisted that my team would master the fundamentals at a level that consistently exceeded client expectations.

I hung my favorite quotes on the walls of my office: Vince Lombardi's "Winning is a habit;" John Wooden's admonition to his players to "Let the other guys rise to the occasion. We'll already be there;" Thomas Edison's observation that "Many of life's failures are people who didn't realize how close they were to success when they gave up." I trusted that The Great Unknown would not put this fire in my heart and then fail to provide the resources necessary to bring my dreams to fruition.

I wasn't always able to keep the vision; sometimes I lost my faith. Sometimes, I still stumble in my faith, only to return to the reality that this moment and the love of the Creator that gave me this moment are all that I have right now. Among other tidbits of inspiration and the encouragement of loved ones, quotes or mantras have helped me stay focused.

Reminding myself several times every day of the opportunity I've been blessed with, the opportunity to rise and compete again for another day, is something that helps me maintain the energy and enthusiasm to welcome life's challenges.

There are seven mantras that I repeat to myself:

"I am surrounded, embraced, protected and loved by the Creator of the universe."

"Health, wealth, love, and happiness abound in my life, and continue to arrive instantaneously in the amounts that I desire."

"Fear, doubt, and indecision kill, but they die in the presence of faith, and I have unstoppable faith."

"I have complete control over my thoughts, and they carry me in the direction of my dreams."

"I embrace uncertainty. It's where all of my potential becomes reality."

"All things are as they should be."

"I am winning with the help of my Creator."

Once, when I made the mistake of showing my mantras to some friends, they chided me for "believing such nonsense." How could I be sure if these mantras were true and why was I so obsessed with achieving certain goals?

In all fairness, my friends had a good point. These mantras may not always reflect reality... but what if they do? Wouldn't that change everything? How might I approach life? What if I just chose to believe that these things are true?

Every day, we wake and assume the sky is up and the earth is down. We assume we live on solid ground that does not move. We believe the sun will rise every day. We believe cloudy days are darker than sunny days. We think we KNOW these things.

Well, guess what? The sun is where it is only for a moment, and it's moving really fast across the galaxy, and it's not up in the sky, it isn't even part of what we think of as the sky. That solid ground you thought was stationary is spinning at twenty-four thousand miles per hour, while the earth is hurled by centrifugal force around the sun. And by the way, the sun doesn't rise; we just think it does because the earth spins and the sun appears to ascend on the horizon. Cloudy days are just as bright as sunny days if you rise above the clouds.

So, who's to say whether my mantras are accurate? I chose to believe in them, and eventually, they led to a series of habits that seem to be serving me well.

On a day-to-day basis, I developed the habit of getting mentally, physically, spiritually, and emotionally centered every day. I regularly and enthusiastically review a series of papers I've had neatly typed and spiral-bound into a personal notebook. This personal notebook soon became the blueprint for my life, and I've continued to update it with goals, action areas, and photos of the people I love most, as well as visual images of what I most desire. This notebook content has dramatically affected my relationships, my business, my health, and probably my future. I call it my *Mission Notebook – Meeting the Challenge*, and it consists of seven sections:

-A Description Of The Person I Most Want To Be
  -My Undeniable and Inspiring Truths
  -Things For Which I Am Most Grateful
  -My Seven Rules

-The Actual Incentives That Drive Me Every Day
-The Destination If I Accomplish My Goals
-The Critical Path To Reaching My Goals

My notebook may appear to be a form of goal setting, but it is not. Probably like you, I've noticed that by focusing on specific goals, some people can improve their effectiveness in parts of their lives, and they tend to move toward these goals. But after having read many books on goal-setting techniques and the importance of goals, I became puzzled by the fact that for the most part, goal setting as a technique, more often than not, doesn't work for me.

The reasons why goal setting often does not work are two-fold. First, most people set their goals without initially considering where they are trying to go. I equate this process to driving fast in the wrong direction and growing frustrated when you don't arrive early. Now, to be fair, goal setting is a process that almost all successful people employ in some form, whether consciously or unconsciously. But successful goal setting works best when it ties directly to the process of becoming something or someone, and it specifically ties to the things that matter most.

The second reason why goal setting often fails is that it is easier to list a bunch of goals than it is to execute a real strategic plan. Several years ago, while preparing to videotape the CEO and founder of a company with more than $1.5 billion in annual sales, I sat in his desk to make sure he would be able to read the teleprompter when we began to record. I noticed a small acrylic block facing me on his desk containing nine goals for the year.

Until that point in my life, I had a "to-do" list that was several pages long. I used to refer to this list as "My Goals". Sitting in the CEO's chair, I thought to myself, "Here I am struggling to pay my bills as I diligently adhere to my list of 'goals,' while this guy is only thinking about nine things this year. And he's a billionaire!" We're all familiar with the concept of simplifying, but how many of us actually practice the idea? Well, now I do!

Step One in setting effective goals is to "know your heart." I believe this concept is the cornerstone to life, and I'll be coming back to it later as a foundation in my own seven-step strategy to "Meeting the Challenge" and "Getting It."

Let me illustrate what I mean by "know your

heart." I am not a person who cries very often. Like all people, I've had to deal with my share of heartbreak: seeing friends go through difficult times, losing loved ones, and sometimes feeling like I am totally alone. I now consider these times to be blessings, as they have helped me to counsel others when they are going through tough times, specifically in encouraging them to find God in every person and every situation, conveying to them that they are never alone, and urging them to make sure that others know they are not alone. But for the most part, these times don't bring out the tears.

Aside from the days my parents died (and even then, it was just for a moment while walking alone) I can only think of two times I've teared up in the past thirty years: celebrating the life of a friend at a Quaker memorial service and listening to the father of the groom make a wedding toast. There is something about the human heart that connects, and when it does, you know it.

Two of my closest friends and business mentors, Andy and Leslie Price, have impacted my world in ways that can only be described as life-changing and miraculous. They are an inspiration, and in fact, an engine that is enabling much of what I get to do. In addition to being two of the smartest and kindest people I know, Andy and Leslie have the coolest family and friends.

One of those friends, Bob Berger, became my business attorney and helped me to set up the legal entity for POC Media. I only got to know Bob for about ten years, which may seem like a while, but it was far too short. When Bob passed away suddenly, his friends and family arranged a memorial service for later in the week.

Having never attended a Quaker service and not being personally familiar with most of Bob's family and friends, I was not prepared for what would follow. For approximately two hours, Bob's friends, probably a couple hundred—and they really were friends—told stories of how Bob had touched their lives. In listening, I realized that my picture of Bob was being completed. We all knew how great Bob was, but I'm not sure if we all understood how he had so personally affected so many people in so many ways.

It was an evening of laughter and tears, and yes, I'm sure that many were crying for the loss of Bob, but I think there was something else going on that night. I think we were also crying because we were witnessing greatness—not perfection, but greatness. We had witnessed a job well-done, a life well-lived.

And something happens inside when you see real greatness in action; it's like basking in the grace of The Great Unknown. Your heart connects, and you are one with The Creator. Personally, when I am humbled by the presence of greatness, I find myself overwhelmed with emotion. I can only imagine how the few instances we find on earth compare to the emotion of confronting The Great Unknown.

Similarly, I attended the wedding of two friends whom I admire both personally and professionally. The groom, Pat Brady, is one of my mentors and the living definition of success—morally, professionally, personally, in every sense of the word. The bride, Jennie Brady, is a kind, intelligent, beautiful person with a great sense of humor, the vulnerability to love, and yet the mental strength of steel; she's perfect!

When the father of the groom stood to give a toast, he calmly reflected on the joy that his children had brought to both him and his wife, and staring lovingly at the happy couple, he smiled and said, "Pat, nice going!"

Those three words summed up the groom's

life until that day: the culmination of a life well lived, love shared, and the natural consequences of goodness. If I hear those words from my own parents when I get to Heaven, I can probably dump a lot of baggage outside the pearly gates. I'm guessing I'm not the only person who feels that way.

So, what do weddings and funerals have to do with setting goals? Everything! Weddings represent the start of a new life together with the person you can't live without. Funerals should represent the space between the starting line and a meaningful milestone. From a distance, we can step back and easily determine what matters most, and it's everything Bob's friends were saying about him at his memorial service. Nobody talked about his wealth or business success, because their hearts knew none of that stuff mattered most.

Our minds, our emotions, our insecurities, our fears, they all tie to what we want now, and these things change with the wind. But our hearts see from a distance; our souls and our love are all we get to take with us when we leave. As the old saying goes, "How much did the richest guy in the world leave behind when he died? All of it." It doesn't really matter how nice the bed you die in happens to be. The sooner one understands this truth, the sooner one uses the heart to set goals.

And the biggest challenge to following one's heart is resisting the temptation to impulsively follow the head for what one wants now. Guys who cheat on their wives, people who become addicted to drugs, gambling, or other self-destructive vices, and businesspeople who milk every last nickel out of a deal instead of nurturing the relationship; they're all putting what their minds tell them they need now ahead of what their heart is telling them they desire most.

Some very intelligent friends of mine question eternal life and the existence of God. I respect their skepticism; how could a reasonable God have allowed the Holocaust, the plagues, and World Wars I and II? Why are some lucky bastards born into lives of affluence, while equally worthy people live in poverty? My own high school, while wonderful for me, was a house of horrors for some students who claim to have been molested by several of the very priests who heard our confessions. Why is there suffering and inequality in a world where God could just will things to be different? Why did my wife's father die at such a young age? And why did someone as compassionate and moral as my mom have to lose her husband suddenly and then spend the last twelve years of her life deteriorating from Alzheimer's Disease and multiple congestive heart failures, only to die from COVID-19? So how does one criticize a skeptic when these questions make so much sense?

As I stated at the beginning of this book, I don't have The Great Unknown figured out, and I certainly don't pretend to be able to figure God out for others. A good friend once told me that she believed challenged people were actually angels, sent here to help us see the best in ourselves when we are compassionate. America rescued Europe from Hitler's terror, and there are people mobilizing to help those less fortunate than themselves every day.

I have a friend named Marianne, of whom I'm a big fan, who established a foundation that has delivered more than thirteen million meals to the chronically ill and home-bound AIDS patients. Her foundation is called Project Angel Food. Even in my mom's suffering, I was able to see a compassionate heroism coming from my sister, her husband, and her kids, as well as from my own wife and kids. I envy the optimism and compassion that enables the beautifully empowering take on life that "angels are here for our learning."

Perhaps I'm too jaded, but I lean more toward the belief in a collective faith that can overcome fear, and I'm counting on an eternal God who will someday provide one of those explanations that will give me the old slap-in-the-head "Ah-ha" moment, like, "Oh, maybe there was something obvious that I was supposed to be doing, something to help those people!"

So, my idea of going with the heart for what matters most and for living my life with the intention of providing my friends and family with lots of great material for their eulogies at my funeral, works best when I believe that The Great Unknown is a loving God.

And my roadmap is most effective if the apparent end of the line is really more of a change in address, followed by a new page. The roadmap for me is built upon core beliefs. My heart's desires spring from these core beliefs, and my goals are a function of both. So now, when I feel like giving up—as we all do from time to time—or when I wonder if it's worth battling on, I hold to a desire to someday understand why every obstacle was worth overcoming. The goals are solid, and they support what matters most: the heart stuff. For me, the way I get there is by staying centered—mentally, physically, spiritually, and emotionally—every day.

The Get / The Recap

I seek out mentors who have moral compasses, expertise in areas that affect the journey toward what matters most, and a desire or willingness to help.

My mentors' qualifications have nothing to do with formal education, religious beliefs, or age. The more diverse they are from each other, the better.

Successful people differ from each other in many ways, but there are some habits that most successful people share: knowing what they want, knowing rather than believing they will succeed, maintaining a focus on what matters most, and never giving up.

Mantras can help keep the most important beliefs front-of-mind.

Showing goals and beliefs to others is not always a good idea. It's best to only share dreams with those engaged in helping one reach a vision.

I always check in on reality. Sometimes things are not as they appear to be, and mentors can help one see more clearly.

A system for repetition can help one stay on target during distracting times.

Goal setting can work, but it's best when it is refined toward the things that matter most.

Being mentally, physically, spiritually, and emotionally centered can help one maintain a focus on the things that matter most.

Chapter 10
Love, Trouble, and the Space Between

Since going into business, I've had the pleasure of meeting a wider variety of people than most. Many of these people, approximately one third, happen to be women. And while my male friends and clients typically like to talk about solving problems, the success of their kids, business, money, and sports, it has been my experience that several of my women friends and clients, many of whom are among the most goal-oriented people I know, like to discuss their feelings. I don't notice this as much from the men I know.

Personally, I'm not very in-touch with my own sensitive side. My wife, Dot, would strongly support this statement. Dot is the most beautiful woman I know—beautiful in every respect. I think she is stunningly gorgeous, kind, compassionate, loving to family, friends, in-laws, and anyone in need; in short, Dot is the nicest person I've ever met, and I love her more than anything. She has successfully balanced motherhood with her career and the challenges associated with being married to me.

Interestingly, my wife doesn't see herself the way I see her, and she has always sold herself short. Having lost her father at an early age, she may have missed the presence of a man in her life, letting her know how special she is. Being married to a man who spends a lot of time on the road, it would be easy for her to have still felt very alone at times.

That being said, I can't remember a conversation I've had with Dot in the past thirty-five years that didn't end with the words "I love you" coming from both of us. Similarly, I can't remember a day going by that we haven't told our children the same thing. In fact, from the time they could respond, I believe both of our children have seen themselves as winners and wonderful people.

It's not that we've tried to condition them this way, but I believe the fact that Dot and I both see our children as winners has caused them to see themselves the same way. And, in fact, by most reasonable or measurable metrics, they both are "winners," loved by many, and successfully pursuing the careers they most enjoy, on their own terms.

Of course, when things are going reasonably well, when Mom and Dad are saying you're wonderful, when there is little to really fear in life, it's easy to see oneself as a winner. But what about the weeks when you're getting hammered by life? How about when someone you trust and respect calls to tell you that your failure may hurt your whole extended family and that you need to quickly ignore your other responsibilities and get ready to fold your business?

What about when the people you love and trust most feel the need to let everyone know that you're not winning and they aren't quite sure that you ever will? What about the day your primary bank decides to call a loan and ask for a big check in eight days, but you can't pay it? Yes, I've been there too! What about the day you find out that someone is spreading terrible, inaccurate rumors about you, and you could be losing clients and a stellar reputation? What about the feelings of failure when multiple advisors suggest you file for bankruptcy because they see no way out of your predicament, even though doing so would harm the very people who had enough faith to back your efforts?

What about when you find yourself sitting in a parking lot in a very bad part of Charlotte, North Carolina in the middle of the night, contemplating the unthinkable, wishing that "this cup might somehow pass from you" and wondering how long you can endure the circumstances? What do we do?

We live in a world of seekers and visitors. Seekers have been there and lived through the challenges. They've crashed their ships on the rocks and climbed out, alone if necessary, to rebuild their dreams and launch them again. Visitors just like to pop in, give an opinion, and walk away thinking they've contributed to the situation. Visitors have nothing on the line; they're just visiting. More often than not, they're not even offering to help. Seekers don't respect visitors. BE A SEEKER!

So, here's what I've found, and to my surprise, I've come to realize that most seekers have experienced the same things. The intuitive answer to all of the above scenarios is to "buckle down" and focus on your challenges and the ways to overcome them; however, I discovered by accident that this is not necessarily the best answer. The best answer was to fall in love.

While I'm speaking somewhat metaphorically and not advocating being unfaithful to one's spouse, the reality is that the journey through my most troubling times has carried feelings that can best be explained as those of a passionate love affair. While I'd readily exchange pain for something that feels better, I can honestly say that the hardest times in my life have produced some of the most precious relationships, and I'm told that in some cases they have changed people's lives for the better. And that is something I would not trade.

Fortunately for me, whenever I've been in the midst of a frightening challenge, fate has found a way to inject me into the life of someone else dealing with a much more serious challenge. Praying for another person is very powerful and may shatter all your illusions of who you are and what's important to you. Praying intensely for another person over a prolonged period of time will cause you to love that person, not in an inappropriate way, but in a way that will definitely keep that person in the front of your mind. This love will quickly become a foundation for your meditations, and it will bring you closer to God. The result is that you tap into the energy—the Love

Power—that brings about your intentions and the solutions to your problems.

Once I realized this, I began praying intensely every day for my wife and children as well as those whose lives I believed God wanted me to touch. I made my prayers specific and powerful, and prayed with certainty that they would be answered. While the answer was sometimes "no," I prayed knowing that God's plan would be better than my own and that somehow my own commitment to love would bring about results that far exceeded anything I would have thought of on my own.

I found that by focusing on God's will (not only in my own life, but also in the lives of those that I could touch) everything just felt right. It caused me to forgive those by whom I had felt offended. And just when I'd hit a point of surrendering to God (because I would honestly want God's will, whatever that might be), somehow, all of the other stuff fell into place.

The image of this Love Power reminds me of a metaphor for heaven that I've heard described by several different people, so I'm assuming it's been around for a while. The metaphor is that both Heaven and Hell are filled with people who have no elbows. They can't bend their arms to bring food to their mouths. As a result, in Hell, the people are starving as they try unsuccessfully to eat their food by throwing it in the air or licking it off of the floor. Malnourished, they cry out in pain and suffer from lack even though they live in abundance.

In Heaven, the people are filled, happy, and loving, as they use their arms to feed each other. Sure, it's just a metaphor, but when life feels most dysfunctional, I'm always reminded to check my elbows.

I have several friends and clients who have told me of their childhoods in what they refer to as dysfunctional families. I use this phrase carefully because I believe everyone is the product of a dysfunctional family. It's just not natural for people to agree on everything, and I believe the expression "dysfunctional family" is grossly overused. When I use the expression, I am talking about a family in which one or both of the parents were either deceased or departed, and specifically those cases where relationships were left without some form of closure.

I have been amazed with the similarity by which women whose fathers went away at an early age and men whose mothers disappeared at an early age view relationships. My experience is that many of the women see men as unfaithful, and see themselves as flawed, both in terms of emotions and appearance, while many of the men I've seen grow up under these circumstances seem to not respect women.

Ironically, the women to whom I am referring are among the most kind, intelligent, good-natured, physically attractive, and successful women I've ever met. They are the women that we all say could have any man or woman they want. Same with the guys. Interestingly enough, all of my friends growing up under these circumstances seem to be extremely careful about using the word "love."

I, on the other hand, always use the word "love." I love my family, I love my friends, I love chocolate, I love the Philadelphia Flyers hockey team, I love Disney World; I love my clients, I love Jesus, I love my employees, I love what I do for a living and the people with and for whom I do it, and at the risk of sounding narcissistic, I love myself. I also find it very easy to love other people as children of God, and I believe this love is made easy because I do love myself.

Personally, I wish more people used the word love more often. It occurred to me one morning while walking through the hallowed hills of Valley Forge that if I knew I was about to die, the first thing I would do is call everyone I care about and let them know that I love them. I would no longer worry about whether it would be perceived as inappropriate, whether women would think I was hitting on them, whether guys would think I was gay, whether clients would think I was sucking up, or whether my detractors would think I was nuts. Perhaps the fact that I have not yet made these calls reveals my own insecurity. Maybe this will be my next project.

A Christian friend asked me five interesting questions once at dinner: What if God is real? What if God is actually LOVE? What if God loves US? What if Jesus is exactly who he said he was? Wouldn't that change everything?

What a beautiful value love is as a foundation for everything else we do. It seems so right, perhaps it will someday seem natural.

PAT O'CONNOR

The Get / The Recap

Seekers bravely attack their problems, while visitors are just visiting. It's good to be nice with everyone, but visitors can be politely ignored.

Our most precious relationships often come during our times of highest emotional flux.

Prayer has power. Praying for those we love brings power to the relationship.

Every person we meet is someone's child.

"What if" is a powerful way to begin a question.

Chapter 11
Boss of Me

We've all heard children say, "You are not the boss of me." Oh, if only we lived our lives that way. Who actually is "The Boss of YOU?" Is it your lover? Maybe your friends? A well-meaning relative who will do anything to help you avoid pain? Your fears? Some bully? The demons of your youth that you can't even understand?

Maybe you were too young to process things going on around you. Maybe your parents or teachers inadvertently burdened you with their own insecurities—sorry Christian and Devon, remember this chapter and do better with your own kids. We carry those insecurities with us through life; some wear them as a misunderstood badge of honor and some drag them like a ball and chain.

I was blessed with amazing parents. There was nothing they wouldn't do to try to make a great childhood and a promising future for both my sister and me. My dad was a self-made guy, the first in his family to attend college. He did it through the ROTC program where the Army paid for school and then he graduated and served in the Army before becoming a professional civil engineer. My mother had been a beautician, and she became a stay-at-home mom within a year of marrying my dad.

Dad's lessons were simple: "life will throw challenges at you and knock you down; you'd better get up and throw some punches. I'm here to help." Mom's lesson was simple, too: "you are unconditionally loved by Mom, you need to be very careful, and I will defend you and support you no matter what." They loved each other as well as my sister and me; two hearts could not have been more in the right place.

As amazing as they were—and they really were amazing—sometimes the two messages could be unintentionally conflicting. My Dad was not careful; he was the son of an Irish immigrant who had come to the United States with nothing in his pockets and nothing to lose: a boxer-turned-industrial-painter with the heart of a champion and a vocabulary right out of central casting.

My mother suffered the humiliation of being held back in second grade, due primarily to an illness that threw her off for several months. She didn't graduate with her friends, and she would spend the rest of her life wondering if people thought she was smart, as if that should actually matter.

When I was growing up, Mom sheltered me. I remember once I was delivering newspapers at 5:00 a.m. on a Sunday with my front and side bike baskets full plus a huge back satchel filled to the brim with copies of the Philadelphia Sunday Bulletin. It was dark and cold, and my bike slipped on the ice, spilling both me and about one hundred newspapers onto Sunny Hill Lane. Mom had been watching from the window and came running out to check on me, to help re-rubber band the newspapers, and to put them in her car to drive me around the paper route that morning.

Mom also volunteered to work in my elementary school library because she knew I was creating some behavior-related problems in school as I kept getting sent to the principal's office. She said it was easier to just walk down the hall to meet with the principal than to drive in on short notice when the inevitable daily calls would come. I think she probably enjoyed the opportunity to help the kids and keep an eye on me as well.

One afternoon, our school principal made a

serious error in judgement and timing. I had done something silly in class and was sent to his office. My mom walked in as he was in mid-sentence, loudly and passionately telling me that I would never amount to anything.

Now, I've seen Mom get angry more than a few times, but never anything like that afternoon. She started hard and only broke stride to tell me to grab my stuff from the classroom; we were headed home. When I grabbed my books and returned to the principal's office, Mom was still in full flight. On one hand, I thought, "wow, she's got my back." On the other hand, I was not looking forward to Act II when we got out in the car. But Act II was very surprising and beautiful.

She was silent, started up the car, shifted into drive, then shifted back into park; and with tears in her eyes, she looked at me and said, "Patrick, you are a good boy. Don't ever let anyone tell you that you'll never amount to anything. You can do anything you set your mind to." And then we drove home in silence; message received.

When I was fifteen, I told my parents that I wanted to get a gig playing in a piano bar. My mother was terrified; she just knew that I would go from bar to bar until someone hired me, and her fear was that I would spend weekends in a bar. Given my Irish heritage and an ancestral penchant for booze, that might not have been a good thing. Dad was amused; he pointed out that I was still riding a bike, that I wasn't a very good singer, and that no bar owner in their right mind would hire me at my age.

I came home that night with a bar gig that I kept for six years through college, adding other bar gigs to my open nights. Nobody was prouder than my father, and nobody was more worried than my mother. I think they came to see me play almost every weekend. Dad would tell me what I should be doing differently and often made fun of my singing, while Mom would tell me I was perfect, even though she liked the Elton John and Billy Joel songs more than those of Little Richard and Jerry Lee Lewis. Truth be told, Mom was really more of a Barry Manilow fan.

By the time I was married with kids, and struggling to stay in business, my mom would pray for me and tell me there would be no shame in giving up and getting a real job. Dad, on the other hand, seemed angry that I was failing to deliver at the level he felt I was capable of. He was right; I was bitter and disgusted with myself too.

One night, after one of Dad's particularly harsh criticisms of my performance as a businessman, husband, and father, I'd had enough. The two of us were sitting in my parent's kitchen, as I had stopped by on my way home from the airport after a tough business trip to say "hi," not expecting a review of more flaws than I was aware that I had.

So I said, "How's the ringside view?" My dad seemed puzzled, so I elaborated "Everyone I know believes they understand more than me about running my business. It's like watching a fight. I'm in the ring, getting my head bashed in while all of the critics sit in the front row yelling 'get up,' 'stay down,' 'duck,' 'punch back.' It's so easy from the front row. Try stepping into the ring. Everything is faster and the punches really hurt. And not only do you get knocked down, but as you're getting up to get hit again, you have to listen to your dad tell you that you suck!"

Finally, Dad explained what I had misunderstood for decades. He smiled and said "Pat, I love you, and I'm proud of you for stepping into the ring. I would expect no less of you. But if you can't handle the criticisms of someone who loves you and roots for you every second, then how are you ever going to handle real adversity? I'm too old to step into the ring and I can't help you with a fight that you alone have chosen. The opportunity to go for the title on my own has already come and gone for me, so I root for you. I'm not going to sugarcoat it when you're coming up short. If you need a hug, Mom's in the other room. I'm proud of you, win or lose, and I'd be proud even if you weren't competing. But you chose to compete, and now that you're in the ring, I want to see you fight, and I'm expecting you to win!" Wow, it took me that long to find out that Dad was proud of me. Maybe that school principal had a point; it sure takes me a while to learn.

So who is "The Boss of You?" The Creator endowed us with free will. I have many friends who have been through the 12-Step Program, and others who spend countless hours in psychological therapy. These processes can be very effective, and they seem to lead to the conclusion that we are flawed creatures, doing our best, relying on something greater than ourselves, but still responsible to assist in our own rescue. There are so many ways to arrive at the same place. We're influenced by our past, by our faith, by our fears, by our doubts, and by indecision. But at the end of the day, we all know the answer to the question "Who is the Boss of You?"

YOU are the Boss of YOU! You control your thoughts. You can let them carry you in the direction of your dreams. You can embrace the unknown with the knowledge that uncertainty is the place from which all of your potential becomes reality. You can focus your thoughts on what matters most with the knowledge that you are surrounded, embraced, protected, and loved by the Creator of the universe. You can crush fear, doubt, and indecision because they die in the presence of faith, and you can choose to have faith. You can forgive everyone who has ever hurt you, without forgetting that evil exists, and without letting them ever hurt you again. You can know with certainty that all things are as they should be, and you were born for this moment. You were born to win!

When we control our thoughts, we meet the challenge. Sorry it took me so long to get to that, but it's a pretty simple concept. When we control our thoughts, we meet the challenge, and WE are the Bosses of OURSELVES.

The Get / The Recap

Everyone answers to someone or something. That something may be fear, doubt, indecision, pain, regret, anger, resentment, or even the child within, desperately seeking love, or at least acceptance.

Love takes many forms, and the messaging can be quite mixed. We forgive our loved ones for any and all of their faults, because they probably did their best with what they had. They were likely dealing with their own challenges. What good comes out of judging others with less compassion than that with which we hope to be judged? None.

The people who love us most will often feel our pain more than we do. This love can take the form of criticism, and at times even mockery. Never give up on someone who loves you.

Ultimately, WE ARE THE BOSSES OF OURSELVES.

Chapter 12
Be Coming

One of my most sage-like mentors is a former bar owner in whose establishments I was fortunate enough to play many times as a young musician. His name is Steve Mountain, an appropriate name for a man who has leveraged his intelligence, hard work, always-growing network of relationships, and passion to create a massive ecosystem that has grown to include the management and career development of rock stars, media celebrities, and professional athletes, the establishment of fitness regimens and facilities for elite competitors, and the merger and acquisition of global organizations.

Much like my dad, Steve has always had the ability to let me know that he cares while also providing unvarnished advice and constructive criticism with the intent of making me a better person. In addition to being one of the most intelligent and conscientious people I've ever met, Steve has always had the remarkable ability to see the game several steps ahead. His faith in the artists and athletes he has managed, combined with his own intuition commands the room.

At a point in my life when I believed legendary figures were always from somewhere else, Steve became a mentor I could look to, relate to, and learn from. Steve did not need to see someone else succeed in order to form his own ideas. Instead, like a chess master, Steve would attract the best in the world because they all knew that Steve could see the entire field and he was already playing well beyond the competition. Steve's wisdom, grit, integrity, and determination brought him the best clients. Steve was kind enough to allow me to learn from him. In fact, I continue to learn from Steve as well as from those within his orbit.

When I made my leap of faith to start POC Media, Steve introduced me to his close friend and one-of-a-kind client, a force of nature who also became my first client and a trusted mentor, a gentleman named Pat Croce. At the time, Pat owned a handful of physical therapy centers, which he grew to more than forty centers before selling the business to NovaCare Physical Rehabilitation.

Since then, Pat has gone on to inspire millions

by going from the training room to the board room, first as the physical therapist for members of the Philadelphia Flyers, 76ers, and Phillies, then eventually as president of the 76ers before going on to write best-selling books, leveraging his fame and fortune to help others lift themselves from mediocrity to the best versions of what God created them to be. Pat overcame injuries from a motorcycle accident that the doctor, whom I interviewed for a tribute video, told me should have resulted in an amputation. He later beat cancer and used the experience to help others battle the disease.

In his current state of grace, Pat brings the peace of a Zen master to the extraordinary wealth of business and personal success he has created. From rags to riches, and from riches to unparalleled impact, Pat Croce is truly a legend, and I've been blessed with the opportunity to witness his becoming for more than three decades.

I believe it was Pat, who is also an international martial arts champion, that first introduced me to the term "Kaizen." Kaizen refers to a Japanese "way of life" philosophy based on gradual and continual improvement. I later read about what I saw as a similar concept, referred to as "The Flywheel Effect" in Jim Collins's best seller Good to Great, which in turn reminded me of a Tony Robbins interview where he spoke about the paradigm of "constant and never-ending improvement."

I remember just after reading Good To Great, I went to dinner with another of my mentors, Joe Tarsia, founder of Sigma Sound, the studio made famous in the 70s for recording such iconic music from producers Kenny Gamble, Leon Huff, and Thom Bell, and artists like The O'Jays, Harold Melvin and the Blue Notes, The Spinners, Lou Rawls, Major Harris, Billy Paul, McFadden and Whitehead, Patti LaBelle, David Bowie, Elton John, Grover Washington, Jr., Billy Joel, and hundreds of other amazing artists. The walls at Sigma needed no paint; they were covered with gold and platinum albums. Sigma was magic, and Joe was the magician that made it happen.

I have spent a lot of time with Joe over the years trying to absorb his wisdom, but this night was special, bringing an epiphany regarding my relationship with Joe and the impact this one man could have on an industry and those that he touched. I don't believe Joe had the opportunity to go to college, and thank God! The man was a genius, and it would have been a crime for anyone to pull him from the amazing trail that he blazed.

As we sat in a small South Philly Italian restaurant, I began to tell Joe about this Jim Collins book I had just read. Joe was adorable; he would politely turn the conversation to something else until it became obvious to me that he had no interest in the book. So we spent the evening chatting about hopes, dreams, family, and projects, and later listening to a couple of hours of new music in Joe's car.

During dinner, I had noticed that almost half of the songs playing in the restaurant were songs that had been recorded at Sigma Sound. Joe shrugged it off, saying "Hey, we made a lot of great music. Those musicians were wonderful." We were also occasionally engaged in conversation with a variety of people who knew Joe and who came over to pay their respects.

Late that night, we drove back to Joe's office to get my car, and as I watched Joe drive away, it occurred to me that Joe didn't need books. His life WAS THE BOOK. As a beneficiary of Joe's wisdom, I was blessed with the opportunity to learn from the person Joe had become, and he was always immeasurably generous with his time and advice. There is no fitting way to say goodbye to a legend, a friend, and a mentor... My last words with Joe were "I love you, and I'm praying for you."

All three of these people (Steve, Pat, and Joe) had started from different points, all from families with love and modest financial bases. They forged their own paths, touched a lot of lives, and enabled others to pursue their dreams. They probably made a lot of money for themselves in the process, too.

I suspect that none of them still needed to be working, but the money didn't ever seem to be the object of their desire. I don't believe money is ever the foremost desire of a truly great person. Money is just the natural result of good business, and good business is the result of vision, hard work, and the commitment to becoming greater. Greatness is a ripple. It hits, it spreads, and it becomes.

It becomes technology. It becomes art. It becomes commerce. It becomes the foundation for greater dreams and for relationships that can change lives and change the world.

My friend Kevin Lyman founded the Vans Warped Tour, creating a community of punk rockers active in improving our environment by drawing attention to, and funding the support of, mental health efforts, anti-bullying initiatives, and food banks, engaging more than five hundred thousand adolescents every year who may have otherwise felt left out of the mainstream. Kevin and his Warped Tour enabled these kids to impact the world in ways they may have never imagined, and in ways that their detractors couldn't even approach. Kevin's Unite the United Foundation encourages fans, artists, extreme athletes, and music industry movers to work toward positive change through the support of local charities and volunteerism. Kevin's and The Kevin Lyman Group's support of mental health, economic, community, and environmental initiatives is both inspiring and measurably impactful.

Impact can take so many forms: inspiration, mentorship, employment, charity. Fred Maltby got tired of corporate politics and started Drexelbrook Engineering, a level controls company that led the industry. A survivor of polio as a young boy, Fred ignored the permanent damage to his body and turned his attention to growing one of the most successful independent process control companies in the industry.

Before selling Drexelbrook for tens of millions of dollars, Fred positively impacted the lives of many of his employees, myself being one. Countless times after Fred's retirement, until his death while in his nineties, I sat in Fred's living room like an apprentice listening to the master. Fred always bet on himself, and he always encouraged me—in fact, often admonished me—to bet on myself.

Once, when I told him I was thinking of giving up on POC Media and taking a job at another company, Fred leaned over and offered me his glasses. When I asked him why he was handing me his glasses, he said I might need them to find my balls... Message received.

A visionary inventor and brilliant task master who made himself available at any hour of the day or night to those seeking his wisdom, Fred created a blueprint for business management and created a politics-free environment that I've rarely seen in other companies. When he sensed that I was growing weary, he would provide that kick in the ass we all need sometimes, generally accompanied by the words, "Get your head screwed on straight, and get clear on what you want!"

Once, when I was in a jam, he even followed up on those words by having one of his ex-employees call a banker friend who had turned down one of my loan requests, and Fred got me set up with a business loan. Now there's some practical motivation.

Practical motivation... we all need it; we all search for it, and sometimes it appears with clarity out of nowhere. When I was in high school, I wanted to get into the University of Pennsylvania, and I knew that I didn't have the grades to be accepted. The motivation was there, but the path was unclear.

My Uncle John told me to go see a man he knew named Dr. Britton Chance, whose nickname was BC. BC won a gold medal in the 1952 Olympics and was awarded the National Medal of Science for his 1970s work in the field of enzyme kinetics. BC was a force of nature who did not suffer fools patiently.

Hearing that he rode his bike to the lab early each morning, I waited by the elevator at 7:00 a.m. to meet him. When I asked for a job, he laughed at me and told me to go back to high school unless I understood how a spectrophotometer worked. Turns out, BC had written a book about spectrophotometers, so I got him to give me a library pass, and I read the book.

Meeting at the elevator the next day at 7:00

a.m., he grilled me on spectrophotometers. When I passed that test, he asked me about oxidative phosphorylation. This same dance continued for the week covering the Krebs Cycle, enzyme kinetics, funnel-freezing, and mitochondria before I was dismissed with the send-off: "Don't come back. I'm out of town next week."

Knowing that someone had to be in charge of the lab the following week, I pitched the interim director, the one and only Dr. Jack Leigh, with my newfound expertise on enzyme kinetics and landed a job working for the Johnson Foundation at the University of Pennsylvania.

I don't know if BC was actually angry with me or just faking it, but he put me through the ringer for disobeying his order not to come back. However, he also provided the platform from which I was able to publish two papers dealing with biochemistry, sealing the deal for my admission into Penn.

BC was tough, he was brilliant, and he changed my life by showing me a world driven by facts, results, repetition, thoroughness, and real science. He also went to bat for me when I was about to get thrown out of college. BC believed in me when the admissions team at Penn did not.

Other than my parents, I think he was the proudest person to see me graduate. It wouldn't have happened without BC.

Knowing that someone you respect is in your corner can make all the difference. Allan Hardin, the GM of Forefront Records, the hippest label within the EMI Christian Music Group, along with Mercury Records' Kim Markovchick, helped me establish an early beachhead in Nashville when the future still felt somewhat daunting.

One night, Allan and I went to a Nashville Predators hockey game, and when we came out, someone had spray-painted profanity on his car in bright pink. Allan's response was the Godliest response imaginable. He just said, "Oh, man!" From that night on, I've never had to wonder if this man walks his talk. As the old saying goes, "The best way to find out what someone is made of is to put them under pressure and see what comes out." In Allan's case, what comes out is love.

The long and short of it comes down to relationships. One of my mentors, a private equity managing partner and founder of several businesses, is a gentleman named John Foster. John introduced me to the concept that "relationships determine results." This is a simple three-word truth that is foundational to spirituality, marriage, business, friendships, and life in general. I've known John for more than a quarter of a century. He still takes my calls, guides me in areas that are foreign to me, and has helped me become a more rounded and hopefully more circumspect person.

How anyone gets through life without a solid "kitchen cabinet" of mentors is completely beyond me. I've been blessed with amazing mentors, and I love who they've become.

The Get / The Recap

Great mentors can come from any walk of life, with any level of education.

Sometimes, the best mentors are not even aware of their greatness.

Money is very important until one has enough money to be comfortable. It's a little like air: when you don't have it, it's monumentally important, and when you do, it's taken for granted. In either case, I have not seen money as a driver of greatness.

Financial success, as well as enduring relationships, are the natural results of good business.

Greatness is a ripple that spreads and becomes

foundational to dreams.

Winners always bet on themselves.

Excluding interpersonal relationships and the need to respect the rights of a person to reject one's advances, the word "no" generally does not mean "no." It means "no, not yet" or "no, because...."

A "no" can be changed to "yes" by determining the timing and the cause of the "no" and committing to overcome the obstacles. It may require several trips to the library to read books on science, or 7:00 a.m. pop quizzes from a genius on a bike.

If you want to know what someone is made of, watch them under pressure.

Always value RELATIONSHIPS!

Life has a way of chugging along whether we notice it or not. Mentors pass away, and all that remains are the lessons and memories. If you love them, tell them... you never know when the last lesson is coming.

Chapter 13
The Heart of a Champion

One sure-fire way to clear a room is to quote scripture, so I don't generally do it. However, if you can indulge me for one verse, I love the Matthew 17:20 statement, "If you have the faith of a mustard seed, you will say to this mountain 'move from here to there,' and it will move." Some refer to this as delusional. I refer to it as "the heart of a champion," not because it's necessarily true, but because it is the only way to accomplish anything.

This is to say that I have asked many mountains to move. Some have fallen on me, some have laughed at me, some have thrown shadows upon me in an effort to intimidate, but some have actually moved.

One of my most rewarding successes came from the most difficult business challenge of my life. A well-meaning employee sold a project to a global confections company. There was a misunderstanding regarding what was being promised on behalf of my company, and the client moved forward believing they had come to an agreement with an officer of my company.

I'm all for closing deals, and the larger they are, the more exciting they tend to be. But this deal carried two major challenges: First, the employee did not have the authority to make the commitments that were being understood by our client, and second, POC Media had neither the technological capability nor the licensing authority to deliver any of what the client expected.

By the time I became aware of what had gone down, the client had already committed to a major investment in the campaign. I was likely to go out of business and lose everything I owned on what I felt confident would be the ensuing lawsuit. My position was indefensible.

Recognizing the gravity of the situation, I broke the project into lanes with the understanding that we needed to deliver on seven key elements to avoid being in breach of a contract that I had not even seen, let alone signed, but to which I was being held responsible.

After reaching out to mentors and entertainment industry heavyweights whose help I would need, I was able to reasonably assess the likelihood of things working out. Each of the seven elements necessary to stay afloat had an approximate 50% chance of working out. So just to review the math...

    50% of 50% is 25%
    50% of 25% is 12.5%
    50% of 12.5% is 6.25%
    50% of 6.25% is 3.125%
    50% of 3.125% is 1.562%
    50% of 1.562% is 0.781%

In layman terms, I had less than one chance in a hundred of keeping my business, my home, the respect of my kids, parents, peers, and wife, and perhaps my marriage.

When in doubt, I figured the best bet was to throw deep. I grabbed the best people I could find to advise me and to leverage their relationships. One of my most loyal mentors, Pat Brady (the guy from the wedding I mentioned earlier), connected me with a big data company whose chairman he knew in Toronto, an organization that might solve the tech problems.

After a quick trip to the Great North, I found that they couldn't solve my challenges, but they did lead me to a Boston start-up that provided enough coding power to handle the landing site requirements, as well as enough emotional drama to make me pull out what little hair I had left. I was at 1.562%.

Friends from record labels introduced me to other record executives and artist managers, and suddenly I was in a position to bring some exciting artists into the mix. I'm at 3.125%.

A very senior executive at one record label miraculously broke protocol with the rest of the majors to enable me to forge a new strategy for gift-with-purchase music delivery. I'm at 6.25%!

A friend from Los Angeles introduced me to an engineer who helped me devise a strategy that would solve what seemed like an insurmountable challenge in online formatting. I'm at 12.5%!

And then came the turning point! Every game has a turning point, a point at which something happens and one team gets momentum. You generally don't see it coming. It's like that thing I mentioned earlier about many of our best opportunities coming disguised as scary giants named Goliath. For me, I would meet the Philistines (the critical challenge) in Redmond, Washington.

A friend from one of my Nashville record label clients had gone to work at Microsoft and agreed to let me meet with his team of engineers to help devise a solution to a stealth tech component of the project necessary to secure insurance which would be required to launch the campaign. I was joined by a team of sixteen Microsoft engineers, passionately committed to nailing down a solution.

After an hour of brainstorming, having spent money that I didn't have to fly to Seattle, I was politely informed that "the best minds in software seem to have no solution yet; how would I suggest that we should proceed?" I could see that many members of the team were checking their watches and wondering why they needed to waste more time. I told them that I needed to use the rest room, and that anyone who didn't think we could solve the problem should leave, and whoever was there when I returned would be the people I knew I could count on.

I then hustled to the bathroom and threw up. When I returned, there were only four people left, and one of the four made a suggestion that changed everything and allowed me to direct the coders to execute a tweak that made the project insurable. I'm at 25%!

25% is not a good probability when everything

rides on it, but something happened to me that day in the Pacific Northwest. I knew things didn't always work out, and I knew the odds indicated that I might go down in flames, but the prevailing thought from that moment on was NOT TODAY. I may worry, but NOT TODAY. I may run out of options, but NOT TODAY. No matter what it takes, and no matter what I'm facing, I WILL NOT GO DOWN TODAY!

As you've probably surmised by now, the last couple of issues were resolved quickly, and POC Media became the first company to ever launch a million-song download campaign. This revolutionary project introduced me to some of the folks I now consider to be my best friends, mentors, and industry advocates.

Since those perilous few months, I've been blessed with the opportunity to conceive and roll out dozens of new integrated brand and experiential marketing campaigns, ranging from the booking and production of more than one hundred concerts at NASCAR and NHRA races to shows in NFL stadiums and NBA arenas. We were able to leverage our tech expertise and success in sports venues to develop a music supervision and licensing system used by many of North America's largest sports broadcasters. We've also been able to develop and execute branding campaigns for more than three dozen global brands.

As we started working with more and more companies, I began receiving invitations to speak at universities and conferences on the subjects of business development, entrepreneurship, value-based life strategies, and the importance of persistently and passionately pursuing one's dreams. In a world where so many young men and women wake up wondering if life is worth living, I consider the college lectures an opportunity to convince eighteen- to twenty-four-year-old students that it is worth it. Every once in a while, some kid at a school tells me that something I said changed their mind, and I'm reminded why we're here.

Everything starts in the heart. They all beat the same way, but when you combine passion with a commitment to NOT GO DOWN TODAY, sometimes you find the heart of a champion inside of yourself. Some of our best experiences start with pain. Some of our best relationships come from challenging experiences. And every once in a while, embracing the unknown, recognizing that it's where all of your potential can become reality, and slinging some stones at the giant can change your life. Your head will tell you it's crazy; that's a giant out there. But your heart knows what you desire most. Paper covers rock, scissors cut paper, and desire crushes giants. Desire, love, and commitment can bring you what you want most.

So, what do you want most? Are you following your heart? You already know the answer. If you're putting relationships ahead of short-term desires, if you've considered life as a finite span of time with which you can make a difference, if you can face death as merely a milestone marker or an event on your horizon, and if you're taking the long view, then you're following your heart for what you want most.

The Get / The Recap

Sometimes, we must actually have the faith of a mustard seed and tell that mountain to move.

Sometimes, we feel like we're walking alone. That's when we need to have faith, walk fast, and wait for that parade to form behind us.

I acknowledge that I may fail, but NOT TODAY!

Sometimes, the toughest times produce the best relationships, and sometimes things actually do just work out.

The long game matters more than the short game.

Chapter 14
The Moment

So why is it so hard for some people to stay on-purpose with their hearts? I believe it's because it takes courage.

I don't recall where I first heard the expression, but it feels like common knowledge these days that courage is not the absence of fear, but rather the management of fear. Similarly, fiduciary responsibility is not the absence of greed, it's the management of greed. Fidelity in a relationship is not the absence of lust, it's the management of lust. And sobriety is not the absence of desire to jump from the wagon, but the management of that desire. Everyone knows that the best way to overcome temptation is to avoid the temptation altogether.

But the Creator blessed us with the ability to react in the moment, and this is indeed a gift. The spontaneity of reacting quickly can save lives. I guess it's something that our brains do. I don't really understand it, but we've all heard about an old lady lifting a car to save a child trapped underneath it, or we've heard stories of life warping into slow motion while people felt controlled by something bigger than themselves.

I had a crazy personal experience in Santa Monica one Sunday afternoon. I was driving west on Santa Monica Boulevard coming up to Ocean Avenue by a restaurant with indoor and outdoor seating, when a large, deranged looking man came running out of the restaurant carrying a young woman who was screaming. I had no idea what I was seeing, but it looked bad.

Somehow, without thinking, I drove my car up the sidewalk and cut him off, at which point waiters came running out to stop him and the police showed up immediately to arrest him, to find out why he was dragging this woman out, and to ascertain why I was parked on the sidewalk within inches of people who had been having lunch.

The whole thing took about five seconds. Even the police were there within about thirty seconds, but it felt like five minutes. Everything had gone into slow motion. Somehow, I missed hitting the young woman, the tables, and any bystanders. I hadn't even made a conscious decision. It was more like I was being controlled in the moment by something outside of myself. That's how fast the brain can work, and that's an indication to me that sometimes the thoughts within our brains are actually outside of ourselves.

There is a concept that is referred to as entrainment. We've all seen it: a flock of birds are flying in one direction, and then suddenly change direction in synchronous motion. Some of these flocks of birds are flying as fast as forty miles per hour. How do they communicate the turn? I always thought they followed the leader, until it was pointed out to me that they all seem to turn simultaneously.

There is compelling evidence of hormonal cycle entrainment among people living in proximity of each other. There are those who attribute healing to quantum entrainment based on the alignment of electron energy phases. Some scientists who support the concept point to electron phasing and the associated alignment of energy.

Without getting too far over my head in quantum physics, let me just say that I have no idea why these things happen. Maybe there are simple explanations, although I have not heard any simple explanations yet. What I can say is that our subconscious minds can move with staggering speed. One of my favorite authors, Malcolm Gladwell, wrote an incredible book about this called *Blink: The Power of Thinking Without Thinking*. It's a great read!

We live in an environment where we are encouraged to think and act quickly. Left unchecked, this habit fosters impulsive behavior. When you couple impulsive behavior with a natural instinct to shun absolutes and bend over backwards to either make or allow for excuses, it is not difficult to understand why it's easy to put one's "heart's desires" on the back burner for the impulsive desires of the head.

I believe that a normal mind seeks immediate gratification and pleasure, while a focused heart seeks joy and happiness. The younger we are, the harder it is to see the difference. When I was young, my parents told me of the wisdom of the elderly. I didn't see it. I saw some old people doing some pretty silly things, and the older they got, the more they seemed to just hang on to memories. I was missing two key points:

1. People that I labeled as "old" when I was young, were not actually that old. They were more middle-aged and were still figuring things out, and some were in crisis.

2. The memories that the real senior citizens were hanging onto were actually polished versions of their past, seen through the prism of people who were closer to the finish line than the starting line, and who wanted to redefine themselves.

One of my older mentors, a wildly successful and accomplished person on every level, once said to me when I was in my thirties, "Pat, I'd trade my past for your future in a heartbeat." And he meant it. Here's the crazy part: he was happily married, rich, and famous in entertainment circles, and at a time when I was financially broke and failing miserably, my friend believed that every desire of my heart was more than a possibility. In fact, he had a sense of certainty that if I could hold the vision, ignore the impulses of the moment, and follow through, I would succeed. At the time, he believed it more than I did.

Now, it's so much easier to see those past moments and decide what we might have done differently. I'm not even talking about guilt or morality. On a strictly unemotional, empirical level, is a moment of anger worth losing one's freedom? Is a moment of pleasure worth losing a loving relationship? Is an isolated windfall worth losing a client? Is a short-term hit of adrenaline worth losing everything? Of course not, and yet, it's the tipping point that changes lives every day.

The most successful people I know have the ability to listen to their minds, step back for a quick and effective analysis, and then move forward within the framework of what their heart is telling them they desire most. Good parents do it instinctively, protecting and loving their children unconditionally. A friend once told me that if our hearts are connected with God's will, then we will treat ourselves as God's children and make the right decisions.

It's an interesting concept to treat ourselves like children. Every time I see an unhoused person or someone down on their luck, I tell myself "that's somebody's kid." If my kids, God forbid, were ever in that situation, I would want someone to treat them kindly. In keeping with the idea of loving others as we love ourselves, I am captivated by the idea of treating ourselves as God's children.

When I was young, I used to watch ABC's *Wide World of Sports*. Anyone in their late fifties can vividly remember the open, "The thrill of victory, and the agony of defeat!" The agony part is where that ski jumper falls off the side of the ski jump. I'm told he was uninjured, but it looks to me like he's getting killed. That image is my metaphor for putting my heart in front of my head.

It's either "heart over head" or "head over heels;" one way or another, I'm prioritizing or I'm tumbling. Every moment, I'm blessed with the opportunity to put my heart's desires in front of my head's impulses, or I'm cursed with the foolishness of missing the moment. So why have I missed so many moments?

The Get / The Recap

Purpose takes courage.

There seems to be a force outside of one's mind, beyond the traditionally accepted power of an individual that can take over when it matters most.

Our ability to think and act quickly can be lifesaving or it can be our greatest weakness, fostering impulsive behavior.

Putting one's heart's desire, the thing that matters most, ahead of the desire to impulsively follow one's head, results in more of what matters most.

Chapter 15
All the Lessons I'm Taught Until I'm Willing to Learn

Why have I missed so many moments? That's easy, it's because of my big, stupid ego and my willingness to act as if an excuse is as good as correct action. UCLA legend John Wooden has always been one of my heroes. One of his clichés (and I'm totally paraphrasing this from memory, so I'm sure I'm not quite getting this right) is that there is no such thing as a good excuse... our friends don't need them, and our adversaries aren't even listening to us.

Seizing the day or missing the moment; it's just so easy to miss the moment and lose control. I've botched up two of the best business opportunities I've ever had by letting my head get in front of my heart, and for years, I made the excuse that it was some other person's fault. Maybe it was, but that excuse didn't fix anything, and it wasn't until recently that I realized I was doing it again and hit the brakes, possibly too late, again! So here is what failure to control one's heart looks like.

There's a famous recording artist that I used to co-manage. I pitched her music and artistry to senior executives at most of the major record labels, set her up in writing sessions with multi-platinum hit songwriters, cobbled together sponsored events with one of the largest global brands in history, and with no compensation or even a commitment thereto, I leveraged every relationship and source of talent to which I had access to try to get her a record deal.

One evening, we had a disagreement on the phone, and I lost my temper. I don't think I said anything that I didn't really mean; the conversation is a bit of a blur now, but in hindsight, the volume with which I shared my opinion was inappropriate. She fired me.

This was definitely the right move at the time, as she went on to land a very powerful manager. She continued on to win a Grammy Award, sell out countless concerts, and I'm assuming she and her team made a lot of money. I learned a lesson the hard way, got my business back off the ground, and life went on. This artist and I eventually patched everything up and rekindled the friendship. Both she and her family are wonderful, Godly people, and they have been, and continue to be, very kind with both my family and me.

Was I right or wrong that evening? Who cares! A few harsh words spoken at an inappropriate volume may have cost me the opportunity to launch a successful artist management company at a point in my life where everything had been spinning the wrong way, and success at that time could have changed everything. Being right can make you feel good, but getting rich can make you feel great! Lesson learned... maybe.

There's a very successful entrepreneur who supervises music for a large television network. She is a good person: talented, kind, intelligent, and she has an admirable moral compass. I considered her more than a client, having dined with her and her husband a few times at restaurants and even at their home in the suburbs of Los Angeles. This person felt more like a friend.

One day, she called me with two quite reasonable requests. The first was that I hop on a call with a successful entertainment attorney whom she felt I could help or with whom I might collaborate; honestly, I don't remember why she wanted us to connect, but it seemed to matter to her. The second request was that I help land a sponsor for an artist with whom she was working.

My life at that point was a little chaotic. My dad had recently died, and I was going through what I now realize was some form of grieving, but it was something I thought I had under control at the time. Many of us Irish folks like to hide the pain, keep it inside, act insensitive and unaffected by it, and then let it boil over, manifesting itself in more destructive ways like cancer, alcoholism, anger, or in more simple cases, a failure to follow through when it matters a lot to a friend.

So, I did what people going through problems sometimes do. I forgot to return some calls and I failed to get that artist a sponsor. This woman stopped speaking to me or taking my calls for more than ten years. I suppose she was hurt by my lack of follow-through at a time when she was counting on me, and ultimately, she concluded that I was no longer worth the time.

Perhaps if I had taken the time to grieve a bit, acknowledged that I was really in pain, told everyone that I needed to check out of this world for a while, and gotten my head back on straight, things would have been different. I guess I thought I was being strong. I suppose I thought I could make up for my failures down the road. Sometimes we don't get second chances.

In an interesting twist, at a point in my life when I had dismissed from my mind all negativity and regrets associated with situations over which I no longer had control, this person reached out to me. I had the opportunity to better understand how my inaction had adversely affected her feelings at a critical time in the growth of her own new business.

More importantly, I had the opportunity to apologize. If I had it to do over again, I certainly would have let her know ahead of time that I was dealing with some emotional problems, and I'd like to believe I would have done a better job. It was nice to patch things up, yet it would have been nicer to have grown our businesses together during those ten years.

So, as I write this book, I'm a few years removed from the death of my mom, and shortly after her passing, I found myself repeating some of the same mistakes I rolled out when my dad passed away: making decisions at a time when I shouldn't and telling someone they are being unreasonable when the problem is probably that I am being less patient than normal. And so, I'm re-taught the same lessons over again, probably until I learn them for good. The only thing more pathetic than me at my worst, is me AGAIN at my worst.

Moments come and go, but the joy of the wins or the pain and damage from the losses remain. What I've learned from watching winners is that often, the difference between winners and losers has to do with the way they keep score. I used to think that guys who brag about how great everything in their life is were annoying and delusional, and in fact, they are probably both—but it's a healthy delusion. The happiest people I know seem to have short, selective memories.

It's like being a relief pitcher in baseball. If a guy hits one over the fence, that's history. If the pitcher is thinking about that last home run, he's going to hurt his neck watching the next few balls fly out of the park before being pulled and sent to the minors.

The gift of a poor memory—or rather a selective memory—is a blessing. The friends for whom I've come up short, those I mentioned in this chapter, know that I'm sorry. I've already told them. One has forgiven me, one eventually did, some may not ever really forgive me, and maybe that's okay. But all of these balls have left the park and are now history.

No lessons are harder than the ones we teach ourselves, and no person is more difficult to forgive than yourself. In an earlier chapter, I mentioned the importance of forgiveness, even if one doesn't forget. Here's the exception to that rule: until we f forgive ourselves unconditionally when we screw up, learn the lessons from the past, resolve to do our best moving forward, and forget how badly we failed, some people will doom themselves to lives of regret and suffering. It's a choice; it's a selfish, but necessary choice. For those of us fortunate enough to have loving and forgiving spouses and kids, it's easy, almost too easy, and we need to avoid allowing ourselves to get away with bad habits.

That's one of the reasons I like to continue to refer to God as The Great Unknown. I'd like to believe that God forgives us whenever we ask, but that's where knowing what I don't know is so helpful. I ignore the scoreboard and just keep playing, but in the event that the scoreboard actually matters, I try to keep improving. The scoreboard isn't there to tell others if I'm winning or losing; it's there to keep me honest with myself. It keeps me re-learning all of the lessons I'm taught, until I'm willing to learn and apply them for good.

Time to shake off the home runs and throw some strikes!

The Get / The Recap

There is no such thing as a good excuse.

Sometimes our failures are the fault of someone else, but until we own our actions, we're just making an excuse.

Being right feels good. Getting rich feels great! To this end, it's more important to be happy than correct. I'm learning to always choose love and to always chose happiness.

It's important to be in the right frame of mind when making key decisions. It's better not to act when grieving, angry, or doubtful.

Never underestimate the power of a sincere apology to mend a relationship.

When a sincere apology doesn't mend a relationship, perhaps it wasn't meant to be mended. People bring their own emotional baggage to relationships. When someone's baggage is too heavy for the relationship, I believe it's okay to wish them well, leave them with your love and peace, and let them go with no regrets.

The only moment that matters is this moment. It's the only moment we can influence.

Chapter 16
Answering the Bell

One of my favorite movies is *Rocky*, the Sylvester Stallone classic, shot right here in my hometown of Philly. For the last round of the fight, Rocky gets Mick (his trainer) to cut his eyelid so he can answer the bell for the final round. I think every guy, on some level, wants to be Rocky. Win or lose, the real champions in life always answer the bell. They are continually striving to accomplish the goal of getting what matters most, enjoying the process, sharing the journey with everyone they can, and leaving a mark.

My mother-in-law, Dora, is a 4'10" version of Rocky, albeit, in my opinion, much cuter. Born in Italy in 1939, Dora endured a pandemic, the loss of siblings at the end of World War II, separation from her husband as he worked to create a home in the United States, and a reunion with her husband followed by his early and tragic death while Dora was pregnant with their fifth child.

As a single mom in 1973 with only a fifth-grade

formal education and speaking only Italian, Dora did what few could possibly have done under the same circumstances. She raised five amazing kids: all now happily married and wonderful parents, two of whom became PhDs, one of whom worked his way from college intern to head of engineering for one of the world's largest fastener companies, one of whom has worked with her husband to become a real estate mogul, and one who excelled for more than a decade as a manager for the largest accounting company in the world before leaving her job to raise our two children and run licensing at POC Media. In addition to raising successful and driven children, Dora also raised kind, compassionate, and giving children who make a difference in people's lives.

What Dora did is unbelievable, and the way in which she managed to do it is both inspiring and remarkable. I've known Dora since I was fifteen years old, and I've never seen her have a bad day. I've never heard her complain, and she has never expressed a sense of entitlement, only gratitude. She is what America is all about when we think of America at its best, and like every champion who answers the bell, Dora exudes the qualities of a winner; she accomplishes everything she sets out to do, enjoys the process, shares the journey in a way that welcomes, includes, and inspires others, and she has already left an indelible impression on everyone who knows her.

When I think of the people who inspire me most by their answering of life's bell, Dora is at the top of the list. She inspires me, and just thinking about her eliminates any thoughts of giving up on a dream or making any excuse for quitting on a mission.

I've been fortunate. I was born into a loving family with great parents and a wonderful sister, I'm married to the nicest person I've ever met, I have two great kids, I make a living doing what I enjoy most, I still hang out with my best friends from high school, I'm healthy, I live in the greatest country in the history of civilization, and I work in an industry where I have the unique opportunity to meet the very people who inspire me most. I've dined with astronauts, rock stars, concert promoters, evangelists, authors, venture capitalists, new age philosophers, and some of my lifelong heroes.

I believe our world's best heroes are the ones who align what they want most around foundations of independence and interdependence. They have missions that are greater than themselves. They enjoy the process and share the journey in a way that brings joy to others, and when the individual journeys end, the mission is built to continue. Some of such missions include: Mother Teresa and the Sisters of the Poor; Billy Graham and Franklin Graham's Samaritan's Purse; Marianne Williamson's Project Angel Food; Deepak Chopra and The Chopra Center; Kevin Lyman with the Unite the United Foundation and the 320 Festival; Sister Mary Scullion and Project H.O.M.E.; Jon Bon Jovi and The Jon Bon Jovi Soul Foundation; Jason Flom and his Wrongful Convictions Podcasts and Innocence Project support; Stephen Covey's FranklinCovey; MONICA's BeHUMAN Foundation.

People who answer the bell don't dive in head-first, they go heart first and never give up. I used to think of these people as "superhuman," but actually, they are exactly the opposite. They are "hardly-human," but rather spiritual in their own ways. The physical nature is there, but their journey is spiritual. The bell signals the challenge to fulfill life's mission, and these heroes—as well as so many unsung heroes—inspire me every day to answer the bell.

When I'm faced with daunting challenges, I remind myself how blessed I am to have the opportunity to compete. I think of Dora raising a wonderful family under circumstances far more challenging than anything I've ever had to deal with. I consider the millions of people who would happily exchange the challenges of their lives for those in mine. I tell myself that someday I will look back with disgust on every time I failed to get back up, and I remind myself that every failure represents one step closer to securing what matters most.

Have you ever pondered the opportunities with which you've been blessed, and wondered if the wasted ones might manifest themselves in ways that will follow you into eternity, questioning how badly you really wanted this life? This is a thought that haunts me daily, but I consider it to be a gift. The thought motivates me to be grateful for this moment and to make the most of it.

The Get / The Recap

One should never underestimate one's power to inspire and make a difference in the lives of others.

GETTING IT

Sometimes the road will make the most unexpected turns to bring us to a place we could never have imagined at the start of the journey.

The ability to compete is a gift. There are no guarantees regarding how long this gift will be available. The opportunity to answer the bell should never be wasted.

Chapter 17
Seven Rules and the Spiritual Journey

My work in the entertainment industry has brought me in contact with a number of people who follow Eastern philosophers. It was one of these friends who introduced me to the concept that we are not human beings having a spiritual journey, but rather, spiritual beings showing up as humans.

As a Christian, I've always seen myself as a human, but when I studied biophysics in college, I remember being intrigued by the concept of dark matter and energy pockets in the universe. In astronomical terms, dark energy and dark matter refer to areas in the universe where matter cannot be measured except inferentially. It's a name often attributed now to the unseen force that causes the rate of universal expansion to increase. The point here is that all forms of energy cannot yet be explained.

Working in the music industry, where sometimes the most bizarre ideas are both promoted and celebrated for entertainment purposes, I have stumbled across a number of people who would talk about spiritual energy on Earth. Some of these people are among the most morally together and spiritually well-intentioned believers that I've met. They are the people who ask for prayers and offer their own with the belief that collective prayer to a creator—or in some cases, just combined happy thoughts—can create good vibrational energy that results in the fulfillment of the group's collective intentions. There was a time in my life when I scoffed at such suggestions, but the older I grow, the more instances I find of results emanating from collective prayer and intentional thinking.

I think we've all heard the opposite as well: examples of people dabbling in the occult, summoning a darker energy, and sometimes getting results that are too close to their intentions to be explained away by statistical probability. For this reason, going back to how I started this book, I don't claim to have the answers. I don't have God figured out, nor can I tell others what they should believe.

What I am comfortable doing is telling you

what I believe, with the hope that it may align with something that you might be searching for; or at worst, it will give you something humorous that can be used to make fun of me for your entertainment. Feel free to do so, you won't be the first!

I work from seven basic rules. I have found that these rules work for me, but not because they are necessarily correct; I'm not sure they are correct, but because as flawed as I am and as prone as I've been to giving in to impulses that were not necessarily conducive to reaching my own goals, I can say that most of the joy I've experienced in my life has come as a result of following these rules. So here they are for your amusement.

RULE #1: God loves us no matter what, and in spite of our failures and best efforts to screw things up, God's favor remains upon us because He/She/It knows exactly what we are made of... Divine Stuff!

As a Christian, I believe that Jesus is who he said he was, for both historical and scientific reasons. That said, the purpose of this book is not to convince anyone that I'm right, but rather to make the point that as flawed as I am, I believe in second, third, and fourth chances, and regardless of the score, the game can always be won.

RULE #2: Fear, doubt, and indecision kill, but they die in the presence of positive faith.

This is not to say that faith is always correct, but just to recognize that fear, doubt, and indecision are all forms of negative faith. This pathetic trio can only be defeated by a field of energy that plays by the same rules. I believe to my core that positive energy in the form of faith overwhelms fear, doubt, and indecision 100% of the time.

RULE #3: The power of our relationships will heavily influence and likely be the determining factor in the effectiveness of our results.

Ruling out the geniuses of their generations... Prince, Edison, Serena Williams, Steve Jobs, etc.... most people can't go the distance on their own. Elton John and Bruce Springsteen are my favorite recording artists; I've seen each of them in concert more than a dozen times. But as amazing as Elton and Bruce are, they are at their best when they've got their bands in tow. If life is a game, then for the most part, it's a team sport.

RULE #4: It all starts in our hearts. Our

hearts know what we want most.

This rule relies to a large extent on faith. Whatever it is that we believe in will drive our hearts for what matters most: Gandhi believed in peace; Malcolm X believed in justice; George Washington believed in liberty; Martin Luther King Jr. believed in equality; and Mother Teresa believed in spreading love and comfort to the poorest of the poor.

These people didn't share the same religion, but they certainly shared the same level of fervor surrounding their faith in what mattered most to them. I believe that all of this starts with the heart. Wherever the heart is, so is one's treasure, or as expressed in Matthew 6:21 KJV, "Where your treasure is, there will your heart be also."

RULE #5: Try as I may, I often fail to pay attention to the desires of my own heart when the impulsive drive of my head tells me to think about today, rather than playing the long game.

To this end, I am always reminded that while my heart knows what I want most, my thoughts will always drive me toward the things I want now. It's critical not to let the impulsive desires for the NOW override the desires of the heart, meaning the things that matter most.

GETTING IT

RULE #6: Sometimes, the most difficult (but necessary) challenge is to avoid the temptation to give in to the impulsive desires of my thoughts and force them to be subordinate to the desires of my heart. Rule six is to avoid that temptation.

Every time I lose my temper, every time I repeat a previous mistake, every time I fail to look for the good in another person, I am breaking rule six. For me, the solution is to exercise self-discipline. So, to whatever extent I can, when I'm tempted to procrastinate, when I'm tempted to let someone else know that I was right, or when I'm tempted to use my voice, thoughts, or actions for the furtherance of anything other than that which might be pleasing to those who are most counting on my success—either on this side or the other side of that wall we call death—I try to step back and ask what my heart is directing me to do.

RULE #7: So, this is the simplest rule. Persistence in one's pursuit of what one wants most is essential.

Since we can never really reach the summit, rule seven, by default, is to never give up. Giving up is a function of faith... Remember rule two? Notwithstanding legitimate reasons, some marriages break up (abuse, infidelity, the realization that these may be two people who should not have married) I believe that a lot of spouses give up on a marriage simply because they stop believing in the magic that brought them together in the first place.

Entrepreneurs give up on businesses because they start believing the prognosticators of doom they see on television every night, and they stop believing in that divine magic that inspired them to start their businesses.

Countries give up on taking care of the citizens who most need their help, on supporting the health of those who can't afford to cover their own healthcare, on providing an education that can prepare children for the future and the challenges they may face, on protecting an environment with which we've been entrusted, and on the belief that a rising tide can float all of the boats and provide everyone with the kind of future that each of us deserves.

And tragically, so many people, give up on life, not realizing that they were about to win the game.

So, I'm back to the beginning again. I don't have The Great Unknown all figured out, I never will, and the last thing anyone wants to hear is me attempting to interpret God for them. I can say without question that while billions of people have made it to Heaven without me, I know of none who have made it without The Great Unknown.

Get to know Him/Her/It, whatever you want to call It; know that you are loved; crush all fear, all doubt, and all indecision; cherish relationships and make them the center of your life; don't let the impulsive desires of your head override relationships; and never give up on the destiny that you were built to fulfill.

The Get / The Recap

Notwithstanding that there may be those who actually do have everything figured out, for the most part, nobody has the market cornered on truth and wisdom.

There is an energy—or what I think of as a spiritual nature—to each of us.

We each have a choice to leverage this energy and spirituality for either good or not-so-good, and that choice will determine the positive or negative impact we have on the lives of others.

There are Seven Rules that I believe can act as the cutting tools for a meaningful and fulfilling life:

#1: Each of us is loved beyond our comprehension.
#2: Fear, doubt, and indecision kill, but they die in the presence of faith.
#3: The power of our relationships determines the effectiveness of our results.
#4: Our hearts know what matters most.
#5: Our heads tell us what we want now.
#6: When the heart and the head act as one, we stay focused on what matters most.
#7: Faith and true love never fail, and champions never give up.

Each of us has been conceived with divine DNA, and we are built for a level of greatness that nobody can take away. It can only be relinquished by our own willingness to give it up. Never give up!

Your destiny awaits you. Life is about GETTING IT!

Chapter 18
WTF… Why The Faith?

Upon completing the first draft of this book, I showed it to a handful of people that I love—people who I knew would give me frank input, who would like to see me succeed, but who would also agree not to hold back any punches. The feedback from a few of these people was WTF (why the faith?).

Their point was that faith is a "third rail" to be avoided, and one of those fuzzy things that cannot be proven. This is a common knock that I hear from many formally educated people who believe in their hearts that they only deal with facts and science. These people who provided the feedback regarding *Getting It* are also among the most moral people that I know, although faith in God does not play a major role in their lives.

Ironically, I am a biophysicist by training with a Bachelor of Science degree from the University of Pennsylvania, the Philadelphia-based Ivy League university that is considered by many to be among the global leaders in the various fields of science. I am also the founder and CEO of POC Media, Inc., a pioneering entertainment licensing, digital marketing, and concert promotion and production company that evolved into a leading source of alternative media distribution, beginning with the development of league-sanctioned in-stadium and in-arena music videos, culminating with the creation of the artificial intelligence and blockchain-supported POC Media Music Supervision and Licensing System™, used by many of North America's largest media companies.

Statistically speaking (and given my background and entrepreneurial business leanings over the past three decades), one might reasonably expect me to be among the last people to rely heavily on faith.

The approach described in *Getting It* certainly does not rely exclusively on a belief in God, but I consider it less than a leap of faith to believe there is something greater in life than any one of us.

Since some of the critics of my reliance on faith are people whom I love dearly, I thought I should end the book by addressing the "WTF" question with an explanation for why I believe what I believe. I also wanted to make sure—and I continue to desire—that my thoughts be useful and not be badgering or be taken in an evangelical way that drives a wedge between good people. I have no desire to push my beliefs on others.

So here is a short, albeit incomplete summary of what I believe, why I believe it, and why faith plays a pivotal role in my life, and the prism through which I see the world.

I was not a history major in school, but I feel relatively comfortable in believing that certain historical figures existed: Julius Caesar, Cleopatra, Genghis Kahn, Alexander the Great, etc. There seems to be a lot of historical and archeological evidence showing that they existed. I have yet to meet an informed person that honestly questioned the existence of any of these historical figures.

I have, however, met several intelligent, and formally educated people who question the existence of Jesus, even though he lived less than a century after both Cleopatra and Caesar, and there is more archeological and historical evidence of his existence than that of either Cleopatra or Caesar.

I've also heard people suggest that maybe he lived and was a good guy, but there was a lot of hype around him, so who really knows? There were nonbelievers back in his day who still testified to the veracity of claims surrounding his allegedly miracle-filled life. Two that come to mind are Flavius Josephus and Tacitus, both Roman historians who would have had nothing to gain by including Jesus in their works. In fact, they would be likely to face ridicule and possibly persecution for testifying to the existence of Jesus, but they still did, and I'm not aware of either professing to be Christians.

It is also remarkable to me, being a committed entrepreneur, that someone could start an organization with the support of eleven flawed followers and one completely treasonous associate, and still manage to structure this kingdom in such a way that it would be thriving more than two thousand years later, unless that person was pretty special. I know of no corporate leaders in today's world that have the capacity to start a company that could last two hundred years, let alone two thousand years.

When asked, Jesus said he was the Lord, the Son of God, and he didn't really leave any ambiguity in defining what that meant. When they asked if he was a prophet, he didn't say to call him that if they wished. He claimed to be the Son of God. Given that he was willing to die an excruciating and humiliating death for what he said and seemed to believe, I'm inclined to take him at his word. I think he meant what he said. I respect the argument that perhaps he meant it, but perhaps he was incorrect. C.S. Lewis wrote an interesting "Liar, Lunatic, or Lord" treatment on that concept.

Some of my friends tell me that God is not real and that everything can be explained by science and a series of coincidences fueled by parallel universes and unlimited possibilities. I'm not sure I could make the case for 0% probability, but my background in biophysics informs me that the number of parameters that need to work together to produce and further support life is somewhat staggering; temperature, humidity, amino acids, pH, enzymes, friendly bacteria, reproductive processes, and cell division to name a few. I've seen the bodies of people shortly after death and I have sat in on autopsies. I don't understand what it is that separates life from the lifeless, but it feels spiritual to me.

More than that, thinking of the number of parameters that must fall within miniscule tolerances in order for the earth to support life—everything from gravity to magnetic fields to water to temperature to our atmosphere, what some call chance or luck—I believe had to have been dialed in. Personally, I would need more faith to believe in overcoming the odds against an unimaginable series of coincidences than I would need to believe in a Creator.

So as an adolescent, I chose to believe there was something greater than me. Then, for about nine years, I went about trying to prove myself wrong by reading the Bible and finding that it is a series of books with a myriad of contradictions. Unlike some of my fundamentalist friends, I cannot take it literally, nor can I respect the hypocrisy of so many so-called religious leaders. As a result, I thought I had found the Achilles' heel to this whole Christian theory.

However, the more I read, the more I stumbled across Old Testament prophecies that were fulfilled in the New Testament. Some were easy to explain away... born of a virgin (who knows?), born of a woman (of course!)... but born in Bethlehem (Micah 5:2)?... Called a Nazarene (Isaiah 11:1)?... Death by crucifixion (Isaiah 53:12)? Keep in mind that the Book of Isaiah was written between 800 BC and 700 BC, but crucifixion was invented by the Persians between 400 BC and 300 BC, hundreds of years after the prediction that Jesus would be executed by a means that had not yet been practiced. And resurrection from the dead (Psalm 16:10 and Psalm 49:15)? These are predictions over which Jesus, if only a good man, would have had no control or influence. Nobody had ever heard of, or even imagined, the concept of resurrection back then.

Just thinking about the resurrection, all of Jesus's disciples scattered when he was being crucified. They must have been terrified and devastated. Having followed this man, whom they believed to be the king that would crush their enemies, they must have suddenly doubted him to be anything of the sort at the crucifixion; in fact, they fled.

Something must have happened to change their minds, to cause them and so many others to be okay with losing everything, being tortured, and being forced to endure martyrs' deaths for this man. I believe that this happening was a resurrection. So that's why I believe what I believe.

Again, I respect the beliefs of those who don't see it this way, and I only provide my reasoning as an explanation for why faith has such a presence in this book. Faith is the foundation for my life and faith brings meaning to everything else for me. In the meantime, life and opportunities continue to abound, and your destiny is waiting for you. You were born with a dream, and life is about getting it.

This book is about what that has meant for me in my own life. I hope some of what I've experienced resonates with you and hopefully inspires you to embrace the unknown with passion, courage, and enthusiasm.

Thanks for checking out my book. I hope we get to meet in person someday, and I pray that life brings you all of the health, wealth, love, and happiness that it can offer.

God bless and GOGETEM!

APPENDIX

The next several pages may seem silly, but one day, while I was visiting a cemetery, I started thinking about how every gravestone represented both a life and a ripple effect on so many other people touched by that life. We may never know the impact we've had on people. We may not even remember meeting certain people, but either by design or by happenstance, we have more influence than we are likely to recognize.

So, rather than making a short "thank you" section, I just started to list people who either inspired, directly helped, or at least made an impression on me. Would my life be the same without some of them? I'm not sure. Have I remembered everyone I should? I'm certain that I have not. And to those I've left out of the list of names below, I apologize. It's not really a complete list, but rather the names that came to mind while thinking about the specific blessings and lessons from past six decades, while reviewing the chapters of *Getting It*. To those listed on the following pages, and to some I may have overlooked, thank you. I hope life brings all that you desire.

All of the O'Connors... Dot, Christian, Devon, Charlene, Mom, Dad, aunts, uncles, nieces, nephews, cousins, and extended in-laws and family friends, I love you all!

All of the Frattarolas... Dora/Grandmom, in-laws, nieces, nephews, cousins, I love you all!

And then there's Mike Abbattista, Jay Abraham, Adam Acone, Jodi Adair, Glenn Adamo, Mark Adkison, Cary Agajanian, Josh Agajanian, Ed Allen, Charles Ammon, Adrian Amodeo, Laurie Anderson, Marty Anderson, Rich Anthony, Terri Anthony, Brad Arnold, Shant Assarian, Ted Austad, Larry Babb, Marilyn Bachelor, Chelsea Bain, Jim Bailey, John Baldi, Mike Baldridge, Glenn Barratt, Dave Barringer, Rayna Bass, Sam Bass, Karyne Bazanno, Eric Bazilian, Tim Beach, Elle Beck, Jake Beers, Chris Baikirch, Elaine Benedetti, Emily Bergsieker, Joe Berman, Steve Berman, John Bianchette, Mimi and Ott Bissinger, Dustin Bixby, Mitch Blackman, Leota Blacknor, Fiona Bloom, Woody Bloom, Steve Bogusky, Scott Borchetta, Kirk Bornazian, Dean Bornazian, Joe Borrino, Sean Bovelsky, James, Angela, & Lucia Brady, Jennie and Pat Brady, Cindy Breme, Dana Brennan, Kathy Brennan,

Victor Broden, Joe Brown, Joi Brown, Ken Bunt, Mike Burch, Elena Byington, Ricky and Lori Byrd, Michelle Byron, Al Cafaro, David Caldwell, Steve Caldwell, Kirk, Anna, Mia, & Jayne Campanella, Jen Campbell, Chris Capaci, Rich Cappelo, Len Carosiello, Megan Carr, Elizabeth Casey, Bob Catania, Alan Cates, Jim and James Cavanaugh, Ron Cerrito, Britton Chance, Jim Chancellor, Billy and Marianne Chapin, Jo Charrington, Margi Cheske, Kirby Chin, Joie Chitwood, Danny Clinch, Ted Cockle, Lyor Cohen, Stephanie and Matt Cohen, Mighty Jake and Kyle Cohen, Lee Cole, Ray Collins, Tommy Conwell, Molly Corson, Tom Corson, Alex Coslov, Phil Costello, Jim and Anne Costigan, Thomas Coulter, Fred and Amy Coury, Steve Craddock, Joe Croce, Pat Croce, Kristi Crocker, Fred Croshal, Mike and Miriam Cudemo, Scott and Heidi Cunningham, Adam D'Andrea, Keith and Jill D'Alessandro, Michael Danese, Melinda Dancil, Dyer Davis, Ed and Jeanne Davis, Jerry Davis, Mike Davis, Tanya Davis, Phyllis DeCongilio, Nicole De La Torriente, Tatiana DeMaria, Marco & Gabby DeRisi, Tom Derr, Cindy DeSilva and Chris, Kenny DiDia, Mark DiDia, Mark DiNardo, Rob Dippold, Mike Dixon, Brian Dolan, Jim Doyle, Michael Doyle,

Anne and Joe Dudek, Bob Dudek, Dana Dudek, Joe Dudek, Amani Duncan, Mike Dungan, Keith Durbak, Christine Edwards, Connor, Olivia, & Duke Eichman, Keenan Eichman & Von Wallace, Mandi Elliott, Christina Elsaden, Joey Elwood, Craig Errington, Ahmet Ertegun, John "Espo" Esposito, Rod Essig, Rob Evanoff, Patti Fallick, Dan Farrell, Lisa and JJ Farris, Anthony Fanticola, Lori Feldman, Linda Ferrando, Eric Ferris, Jessica and Jim Fickenscher, Dr. David Fish, Johnny Five, Bruce Flohr, Rori Floyd, Alison Flom, Jason Flom, Mike Flom, Reed Foley, Steve Ford, Lionel Forrester, Mark and NJ Forsythe, Fletcher Foster, Albert & Paula Frattarola, Anthony Frattarola, Dan, Judy, Grace, Gianna, & Belle Frattarola, Dora Frattarola, John Foster, Brad Fox, Liz Fraim, Bob Frank, Wolfgang Frank, Mark and Laurel Fried, David Fritz, Heather Gallagher, Richie Gallo, Fred Gaudelli, Jack Gavin, Denise George, Kyle Gerhart, Kristi Gibson, Eva Gilleland, Brad Gillis, Joel Gingras, Marc Giordano, Piero Giramonti, Ward Glassmeyer, Diane Goff, Steve and Jude Goff, Marianne Goode, Kerry Gordie, Rob Gordon, Tom Grabowski, Steve Graham, David Grant, Heather Greene, John Greenstine, Julie Greenwald, Jim

Greenway, Steve Griesemer, Dominic Griffin, Jeff Griffith, Larry Griffiths, Wendy Griffiths, Bob Groux, Phil Guerini, Rolf Haag, Camille Hackney, Bobby Hacker, Tally Hair, Ward Hake, Ryan Halkett, Greg Ham, Bryan Hammond, Allan and Shauna Hardin, Taylor Harlow, Jeffrey Harlston, Dionnee Harper, John Hazelgrove, Terry Hemmings, Tyler Head, Tom Hembree, Chris Henderson, Julia Henry, Marianne Herman, Angie Hicks, Jeff Hillegass, Paul Hitchman, John Hoey, McKenzie Hollenbaugh, Matt Holmes, Chris Holt, Frank Holt, Leigh Holt, Rob Holt, Bill Hooker, Brooke Hopkins, Phil Horvath, Heather Hucks, David Huff, Jerry Hughes, John Huie, David Hyatt, Rob Hyman, Dave Hynes, Peggy and Olivia Iafrate, Mitch Imber, Attique Iqbal, Zach Iser, Rob Jacobs, Larry Jacobson, Nick James, Russ Jenisch, Buddy and Renee Jobe, Erik Johnson, Doug Johnson, Jef Lee Johnson, Barbara Jones, Leigh Jones, Jim Jordan, Kim Kaiman, Rana Kaplan, Matt Kapuchinski, Rory Karpf, Bob Kaufman, Tom Keifer, Kari Keller, Jeff Kempler, Bill Kennedy, Janine Kerr, Tyler Key, Trevon Kezios, Stacie Kinder, Bruce Kirkland, Janet Kirkley, Tim and Kimberley Kleczka, Ben Kline, Randy Knighton, Lizanne Knott, Bruce Kramer,

Shauna Krikorian, Drew Lam, Mike Ladd, Eric Lambert, Eric Laster, Pat Lawrence, Keith Lazorchak, Jack Leigh, Ian Levitt, Mike Sr, Mike Jr, & Lisa Lewis, Kevin Liles, Abby Lin, Jon Litner, Ken Litzenberger, Carmen Liu, Eric Long, Tom Lord, Phil Loutsis, Steve Love, Adam Lowenberg, Vane Lucas, Bob Lucchesi, Josh Lupu, Kevin and Fran Lyman, Stan Lynch, Cindy Mabe, Aimee Mack, Nick Magliochetti, Mr. & Mrs. Ron Magliochetti, Fred Maltby, Lew Maltby, Nick Mammola, Kim Markovchick, Peter Markovitz, Carianne Marshall, Ed Martin, Larry Martinek, Armany Mathias, Amy Matusek, Larry Mattera, Mary and Jim McBride, Greg McCarn, Gemma McInturff, Toby McKeehan, Bob McLynn, Chris McNelis, Dionna McPhatter, Ellis Melillo, Rob and Carolyn Melillo, Christina Meloche, Bob Mercer, Larry Mestel, Phil Metz, Ed Miersch, Tim Miles, Mark Miller, Morgan Mills, Claude Mitchell, Greg Mizii, Andrew Monastra, Moo$h Money, Monica, Silvia Montello, Joy Morgan, Jeff Moskow, Monica Morgenthal, MJ Morse, Shelley and Ron Morris, Susan Moss, Jerry Moss, Steve Mountain, Jack and Cindy Mullen, Jonathan Munz, Michael Newman, Jennifer Nicholls, Hunter Nickel, TJ Nickerson, David Nieman, Nat Nissim, Steve

Norris, George Nunes, Bill and Linda Nystrom, Steve Ochs, Brendan O'Connell, Charlene O'Connor, Jim and Marie O'Connor, John and Cindy O'Connor, Leo and Betty Anne O'Connor, Mickey and Kitten O'Connor, Norman and Joan O'Connor, Rosemary O'Connor, Brad O'Donnell, Mike O'Donnell, Pat and Alicia O'Grady, Chuck Oliner, Amanda Oliver, Mike O'Neill, Barbara Orbison, Christian Orellana, Guy Oseary, Danielle Owens, Jennifer Paige, Lisa Palleschi and Jared, Ralph and Lucy Palleschi, Dom Pandiscia, Mikell Parsch, Jo Jo Pastors, Chloe Pearson, Ray Pennacchia, Jessi Peralta, Frank Perez, Doug Perlman, Tracy Perlman, The Perry Family, Marcus Peterzell, Andy Pfeiffer, Steve Phelps, Keith Piazza, Mark Piazza, Yves Pierre, Mark Pinkus, Rich Pinola, Dan Pitts, Lou Plaia, Hudson Plachy, Rob Poznanski, Bud Prager, Evan Prager, Jeff Preston, Matthieu Lauriot Prevost, Alison Price and Family, Andy and Leslie Price and Family, Matt and Suzanne Price and Family, Suzy Quan, Chase Ramirez, Robert Randolph, Anthony Rankin, Joe Rapolla, Jeff Raspe, Stephanie Raspe, David Ravden, Mike and Kristan Reading, Christine Reimel, John Reliford, Bruce Resnikoff, Rob Reichley, Kelly Rich, Tom and Eileen Richards, Rod Riley,

Mark Rittenberg, Anne Rittenhouse, Bill Roberts, Jim and Linda Robinson and Family, Marc Robinson, Mike Robinson, Rich Robinson, Scott Robinson, Greg Rogers, Joe and Nancy Romano, Wendy Romano, Andrew and Charlotte Roomberg, Paul Roper, Jose and Mary Roque, Heidi Rose, Johnny Rose, Larry Rosen, Charlie Rosenzweig, Ira Rosenzweig, Rosie, Randy Ross, Tom Rowland, Beth Rutt, Phil Sandhouse, Dave Santaniello, Daniel Savage, John and Rebecca Scargall, Madelyn Scarpula, Stephanie Scarpula, Chris Schafer, Mateo Scher, Teresa and Jim Scherer, David Schindler, Dave Schonauer, Deb Schwartz, Tyler Schwartz, Leon Schweir, Sean Scolnick, Ben Scott, Reggie Scott, Chad Segura, Cynthia Sexton, Tony Seyler, Tyler Sgro, Alan Shapiro, David Sharpe, Randy Shefer, Sam Shen, John Scher, Kate Sherlock, Justin Shukat, Matt Signore, Derek Simon, Jayne Simon, Sean Simmons, Aaron Simon, Cindy Sisson, Kevin Sitaras, Allison Skiff, Billy Smiley, Marcus Smith, Robert Smith, Mr. Ed Snider, Robbie Snow, Rob Souriall, Fran Spadaro, Michael Stanfield, Nathan Spang, Patti Spaniak, Kayla Standring, Jim Staples, Mike Stashik, Steel Field Folks, Melissa Stern, Chris Stevens, Steve Stewart, Glenn Stilwell, Jeff

Straughn, Peter Strickland, Howard and Betty Stross, Steve Stum, Chris Sullivan, Frank Supovitz, David Sylvester, Ronn Tabb, Beth Tallman, Jackie Tannenbaum, Joe and Ceil Tarsia, Andy Tavel, Don Terbush, JoAnne Terrell, Kate Tews, JT Thomas, Kim Thomas, Paul and Beth Thompson, Larry Thorne, Livia Tortella, Craig and Denise Townsend, Jim Trace, Lee Trink, Kate Truscott, Nick Turner, David Ullendorff, Jacob Ullman, Geoff Ulrich, Ferdy Unger-Hamilton, Dave Uosikkinen, Matt Varga, Heather Vaughan, Dane Venable, Melissa Verille, Fred Vodde, Corey Wagner, Thomas Wainwright, Brenda Walker, Mat Walsh, Greg Walter, Frank Wates, Lucie Watson, Kelly Watters, Kevin Weaver, Ben Weeden, Julia Weiner, Mat Welch, Holly Wheeler, Megan White, Kevin Wilson, Jeff Williams, Nina Williams, Tom Williams, Marianne Williamson, Kelly Wister, Brandon Witcher, John Wodarek, Daryl Wolfe, Eric Wong, Marc Wood, Pat Wood, Pat Woods, Ruth Wyatt, Erika Zafiriou, and Sandra Zietara.

Thank you all for the wisdom, the lessons, the inspiration, and the love, or for whatever happy, sad, transformational, or just plain memorable elements you've brought to my life.

© 2024 Pat O'Connor

ABOUT THE AUTHOR

Pat O'Connor has spent the past three decades developing POC Media, Inc. into one of the entertainment industry's most innovative integrated brand marketing companies, as well as a leading source of alternative media distribution.

From pioneering in-arena and in-stadium entertainment services to the more recent creation of A.I. and blockchain-based software solutions used to secure and optimize music and intellectual property rights management, POC Media has developed a unique niche that extends across the music, branding, broadcast, and sports worlds.

Leveraging technology and a powerful network of relationships, POC Media has created a high-tech, high-touch ecosystem that includes relationships with most of North America's leading sports broadcast, cable, and streaming outlets as well as record labels and publishing companies. Supporting collaboration among content providers, brands, and rights-holders, POC Media has licensed more than twenty thousand songs, generating millions of dollars for rights-holders in sync licenses, while the event arm of POC has managed the production of hundreds of concerts, conventions, and brand marketing activations.

Pat is a graduate of the University of Pennsylvania with a Bachelor of Science degree in biophysics. He has been happily married for nearly four decades, is the father of two grown children, and lives in the suburbs of Philadelphia.

https://pocmedia.com/

www.ingramcontent.com/pod-product-compliance
Lightning Source LLC
Chambersburg PA
CBHW070054080526
44586CB00013B/1052